Mary A. (Mary Andrews) Denison

Captain Molly

Or, The Fight at Trenton

Mary A. (Mary Andrews) Denison

Captain Molly
Or, The Fight at Trenton

ISBN/EAN: 9783337149048

Printed in Europe, USA, Canada, Australia, Japan

Cover: Foto ©ninafisch / pixelio.de

More available books at **www.hansebooks.com**

OR,

THE FIGHT AT TRENTON.

By MRS. M. A. DENISON,

AUTHOR OF "FLORIDA," "RUTH MARGERIE," "MAD HUNTER," ETC., ETC.

LONDON:
GEORGE ROUTLEDGE & SONS,
THE BROADWAY, LUDGATE HILL.

CAPTAIN MOLLY.

CHAPTER I.

THE HESSIAN COMMANDER.

"WELL! we have driven them this time, General!" cried a red-faced colonel, entering the tent of the Hessian commander, Colonel Rahl, General by brevet.

"Yes, so I should think," replied the General, gloomily.

"You—you are not wounded, General?"

"Wounded! ten thousand furies, what do you mean?" indignantly demanded General Rahl.

"Pardon me, General. I really thought you looked pale—pardon me."

"You can retire," said his superior; and as the younger man left the tent, placing a communication, which the General had required, upon the table, the latter threw down two letters, and then sank angrily into his seat.

"Audacious little rebel!" he muttered, his face growing blacker as he thought, "to write me a note like that."

Meanwhile the offending paper, pure and white, touched only by the delicate pen that a graceful hand had wielded, laid half folded, as he had thrown it down. The other letter, or note, which accompanied it, was written with bolder characters and blacker ink. It ran thus:—

"Dear General,—May I have the pleasure of seeing you at Walsingham House on the 26th? We have all been rejoicing over the late news—thank God and the

King! You have done nobly, and we propose, in a small way, to celebrate the victory.

"LADY JOHANNA WALSINGHAM."

"Who's Lady Walsingham?" the General had muttered to himself, as he threw down this second missive. "Oh, I have it! She must be the aunt of Lieutenant George, in the King's Guards. It won't do to slight her invitation; and yet, upon my word, I feel as much disinclined to pleasure-taking as if I were going to my father's funeral. Well, who wants me now?"

"Corporal Dave has come to see if we shall take the old meeting-house for an hospital," said the guard, as he saluted.

"Take anything that will answer the purpose, and don't bother me; that's not my business," was the sharp reply.

Just then, his servant came in to set the table, and General Rahl, lifting his letters, deposited them, one in his right hand vest-pocket, the other in his left, and sauntered out.

It was now somewhere about six, and the camp-fires were beginning to be lighted. A great many of the officers and soldiers had possessed themselves of quarters in Trenton and across the little stream, "Assumpinch Creek," as the people called it, in the south part of the town. The inhabitants thus suddenly found their houses encroached upon by the Hessians, and, of course, could do nothing but submit. But General Rahl preferred his tent, and so did many of the commanders, for at this time there was a large force quartered at Trenton—larger than it would have been possible to accommodate.

As the General moved out alone, and walked down the regularly-laid street between the rows of tents, the sunlight was fading from the west. The day's work had not as yet occupied his mind. It was only a skirmish of the advance, and by no means a heavy or serious battle. A few scores only on both sides had been killed and wounded, and the Hessians won the victory because of superior numbers.

Misunderstandings at such times will occur, and one had happened that day. The regular forces of Washington's army were expected, and through some signals, not intended to deceive, the small body of American soldiers had begun the work. It was, however, a short fight. Washington's main force did not come, nor was it in any near vicinity. The Hessians magnified their victory. Many of them were fresh—among them General Rahl's division.

The General was a man of imposing stature, fully six feet tall, and proportionately stately. By many he was considered a handsome man—especially so by the ladies. Few men had more noble qualities than he in any ordinary position. But there were cases where his determination changed to stubbornness, his chivalry to cruelty. He was a man who knew no mercy where he conquered. His passions were fierce :—he loved with ardour; he hated with zeal. He despised the Americans as a people, and often spoke of them with contempt, both men and women—at least, until he met Elsie Vernon.

It was a curious meeting.

General Rahl sometimes went to church. One Sunday, as he was passing up the aisle, he dropped his glove. In stooping to pick it up, his sword, as he imagined, touched some one, and he turned, in his own haughty manner, to apologize. The sight that met him struck him with instantaneous confusion.

A richly dressed young girl, nobly beautiful, smiled as she endeavoured to detach her lace shawl from a point of the General's accoutrements. It was over in a moment. The General sat in his pew, conscious of but one thing—that he had seen the loveliest face he had ever looked upon, and also that that glance had sealed his fate.

Elsie passed on with as stately a mien as any he had ever admired in Germany's beautiful women. Her pew was bewilderingly near. Well for him that she was exceeding devout—for to Eslie Vernon her religion was everything. Otherwise she might have marked the great General as rude.

A strange, consuming passion had this American beauty awakened in General Rahl. By the merest chance, it seemed, he met her twice afterwards, once at the house of her brother-in-law, a fierce little Tory, and once at a small party given by one of the aristocrats of Trenton. On both occasions he was near her, and they conversed together. He became more and more enamoured, until he dared to address her by letter, and on the eve of this skirmish he had received, by the hands of her black servant, a characteristic note, in which she boldly and delicately asserted her opinions, and concluded by requesting that the acquaintance might be dropped.

The General's dark eyes dilated as he read it—so did his high-bred nostril. This American girl—one of the people—a girl without rank, or possibly riches—with only her beauty and style to recommend her, had as good as refused him, General Rahl, Commander of all the Hessian forces. It was audacious and should be repented of.

In a very gloomy mood, then, the General walked through the lines of tents until he came to an open spot of ground, picturesque in knolls and tufts of frozen grass and beautifully-disposed chestnut trees, whose bare branches were strongly defined against the red of the evening sky.

CHAPTER II.

THE PRESENCE OF RANK.

As he paused here, an officer was seen coming from an opposite direction. Exchanging salutations with his superior in command, Colonel Dauphney stopped for a moment to throw a glance around.

"I have been on a tour of inspection," he said, hastily, "to the little old church over there. I find the wounds pretty serious, more so among the rebels than our own men. Did you hear, General, that Colonel Wasp has in his charge an important prisoner, a lieutenant-colonel, I think, of the American army?"

"It is very strange—no," said the General.

"In the confusion, and Colonel Wasp himself having received a somewhat troublesome wound, I presume they have neglected to inform you. I judge, however, that yonder is the prisoner, and they are conveying him to your tent."

The General raised his eyebrows, as he saw in the distance a guard, in the middle of which walked a tall, finely-proportioned, soldierly man, in the American uniform.

"He can wait," he said, in an undertone, and then cast his glances about him.

"That's a fine residence;" and he pointed in the

direction of a dwelling upon which the setting sun threw a splendour quite unequalled for beauty by anything he had ever seen in his own country. "It must be acknowledged," he said, "the climate is purer, the air clearer, in America; hence objects in their colouring are more vivid. Whose house did you say?"

"That? Oh! Lady Walsingham's fine place—the finest and most like home I have yet seen in this country," said the colonel. "Lady Walsingham is a widow, I believe; very dashing and handsome—at all events, very showy. She's rich as Crœsus, they say, and decidedly 'one of us.' There's a great entertainment at her house to-morrow night week—let me see—that's the 26th. Of course, you go?"

"Not at all sure of it," responded the General.

"We count upon having a great time. The widow does things in style, they tell me. In this barbarous country, one needs to see something of civilization sometimes, or one would relapse into barbarism. I shall go, if it were only for the purpose of catching one glance at her niece. You must have heard of her—an extraordinary young girl, brought up in seclusion and the utmost rigour of conventionality, and yet she has espoused the abominable cause of the Colonists. There have been whisperings of a rebel lover, too. But, upon my word, Miss Elsie Vernon is the most remarkably superb young lady I ever saw in my life—a crystallization—"

"Miss Vernon her niece!" exclaimed General Rahl, halting, for the two gentlemen had been walking a short distance together, and his face had changed white with sudden emotion.

"I hear it is so," said the colonel, who knew nothing of the General's infatuation, but was impressed by his manner. "Lady Walsingham herself is, or has been, a remarkably beautiful woman I have heard; so I suppose her niece is a younger and more superb edition. Have you seen her?"

"Yes, I have met her once or twice," replied the General, recovering his composure. "She is very well looking—very well looking indeed; rather superior to most of these American young women. But is she like— ah! You told me she was intensely a rebel at heart, I think."

"So says rumour," replied the colonel.

"Pity, pity," muttered the General, "so very beautiful a girl. Has she been long in this country, I wonder?"

"Long? Why General, she was born here. Her father was the Governor's secretary some years before he died, and a very fine gentleman he was, as far I can hear."

"It strikes me I have heard of this Lady Walsingham —I think you called her—abroad."

"It may be so; I have heard very little about her myself till to-day. I shall at all events attend her party."

"So shall I," said the General, grimly, to himself; but, bidding the colonel good evening, he hurried to his quarters.

Supper despatched, he was informed that the one prisoner of importance who had been captured was in a guard-tent, awaiting his pleasure.

"Let him be brought in," said the General.

In a few moments the officer stood before the Hessian commander, fully his equal in all respects save that of rank.

Lieutenant-Colonel Washburn was very nearly as tall

as General Rahl, and even more gracefully proportioned. The General was broad of shoulder and somewhat protuberant of stomach. The lieutenant-colonel was of a fine breadth, also, but more delicately waisted. His eye, larger and darker than that of the man before him, never quailed as its penetrating glances fell upon its captor. In features, he was not as massive as the foreigner, and his full, curly, glossy beard gave to his face an additional beauty.

The two men stood for a moment surveying each other.

"So, you have been taken in arms against your lawful Sovereign," said the General, sternly.

"I consider that I have been taken prisoner by the chances of war, while lawfully fighting for my country, General," was the reply.

"Your country," said the other, with a curling lip; "rubbish!"

The dark eyes of the American gleamed with the fire that shot from his heart at that speech.

"If I were not a prisoner, General, no man should say that to me and live!" he exclaimed, hotly.

"But you are a prisoner."

The young man hung his head. Almost for the first time he seemed to realize his true position, and his cheeks glowed.

"You are a prisoner, and I am one who tolerates no impertinence from the enemies of my King."

The lieutenant-colonel said not another word; and presently the General ordered him to his tent.

CHAPTER III.

MOLLY PUTNAM.

IN a neat little anteroom, leading out of the handsome boudoir of Lady Walsingham, sat a young girl, her hands folded listlessly upon her lap, her eyes humid and red, as if she had shed secret tears.

She was not beautiful, this Molly Putnam, but a right cheery, pink blossom-cheeked damsel, a farmer's bonny daughter. She seemed very deep in thought as she sat there, for her glances looked far beyond the range of objects that bounded her vision. The room, shining in the cheery sun of a clear December day, was much brighter than its occupant, for all its pretty furniture was covered or bordered with pink French chintz, and two or three mirrors reflected back the myriad sun-rays that came in from the quaint, many-paned windows.

"It was mean, that's just what it was, to take advantage of such a handful," cried Molly to herself, shaking with suppressed rage; "but that's just like those great hulking redcoats. And now who knows but poor Paul lies there in the hospital? It chills me to the heart to think of it. He's not dead, for Joe managed to see all of them, poor fellows! Dear, dear, how shall I contrive to find out for myself? I have it," she cried, a moment after, brightening. "I'll pretend to come round to their side. All's fair in love or war—and I must find out if Harry is there, or I shall fret myself to death."

At that moment a silvery sound tinkled near. Molly sprung to her feet, and passed out lightly into the next room. Everything there bespoke the utmost elegance of taste, and a lavish expenditure. The curtains, which let the light in faintly, were of rose-coloured silk; over them swayed the finest webs of costly lace. In the yielding carpet the foot sunk readily; the atmosphere was redolent of fragrance, the most subtle and delicious; while, in an immense easy-chair, quaintly covered, sat the mistress of all these splendours, her luxuriant hair falling spray-like over her shoulders, and adhering to the velvet covering of the chair.

"Molly, I'm somewhat late, child; I was so much interested listening to the news, that my dressing hour went by unheeded. Glorious news, Molly, for us!"

"So I should think, indeed," said Molly, cheerily.

"Should you, child?" and Lady Walsingham, turning round with rather more than her usual vivacity, fixed her bright eyes on Molly's face. The girl did not quail, she even smiled cheerfully, bravely, while her heart was aching, and the lady fell back in her chair, quite elated.

"I thought we should have you, my dear," she said, gently. "The fact is, I shall feel easier in my mind if you really have got to looking at things as you should. To tell the truth, I should have felt some little annoyance at having such a staunch little rebel about my person, much as I respect your good father, who is loyal to the heart's core. I knew it would not take long to bring you to your senses." Pretty Molly smiled. "Now be sensible, little one, for visitors may arrive any moment, and I should not be surprised at all if some of the officers were to come in this morning."

Lady Walsingham was a handsome woman, though nearer forty than thirty. Still she had little need to heighten her charms by art. Her eyes were large, black, and almond-shaped, but almost too brilliant to be beautiful. To features of extreme delicacy, nature had added a complexion of unusual richness, showing that creamy, almost transparent tint, so rarely seen in connexion with a dark skin.

Molly was partly lady's maid, partly companion. The daughter of one of the neighbouring farmers who wished to serve the King's cause, she was too well educated to work in a menial capacity, but her father consented that she should fill the place she did. Lady Walsingham was not hard to please, and the brilliant little country girl was so pretty and witty that she was allowed almost the privileges of an equal.

"Do be quick, Molly, there's a darling. I know I shall have callers—I feel it in my bones. There! A knock, as sure as I'm a sinner—or at least three of them; and—oh! finished have you? Well, you are a blessing!"

A servant entered with a card on a small silver waiter. Molly took the card, as the lady's hands were engaged just then, and her mistress read it over her shoulder.

"General Rahl! Why that's delightful! I certainly never expected him. Molly, tell me, do I look my best—my very best, mind? Which mantle shall I wear—blue, black, or crimson?—pray tell me. One might know I had been among the heathen by my miserable indecision."

"Wear the crimson. There! you never looked better in your life."

"Little flatterer!" cried her ladyship. "Now, take your book, and the blue mantle on your arm, in case I should complain of the cold, you see;" she laughed.

Molly did as she was requested; put on her demurest face, as Lady Walsingham's companion, and threw the mantle over her arm.

"If you could but do me one little favour," she said, pleadingly, as she left the room.

"Well, what! Speak quick, Molly."

"Only to ask the great General if I might be allowed to see the hospital. I never looked upon such a sight in my life. You know I could carry some refreshments for —our men."

"And why not for any of them?" spoke up Lady Walsingham. "I'm sure, although I hate the enemies of my King, I'd do my best for them if I saw them wounded. Yes, Molly, I am almost sure of his acquiescence. Come along."

General Rahl arose as Lady Walsingham sailed into the parlour. He was really astonished at her beauty. Molly Putnam stole quietly into her usual seat, and occupied herself with her book and her knitting alternately. Lady Walsingham, whose manners never had been distinguished by any peculiar reticence, at once glided into easy conversation, and the General thought that if he had not seen the niece, he might have been fascinated by the more mature charms of the buxom, beautiful widow before him.

"Allow me to congratulate you, General, on your victory," she said, after a few preliminary remarks.

"Thank you, though really it was a small affair," was the reply. "A little party of volunteers engaged a mere corporal's guard of my regulars, and the poor fellows got worsted."

"Was it nothing more than a skirmish?"

"Not much more, I assure you. There are less than a hundred wounded in our hospital. You are aware that the church has been taken for that purpose, I suppose? —we have to do these things in times of war—and not more than fifteen or twenty were killed in all. The fellows were foolhardy to attempt the thing at all."

"Poor souls!" said Lady Walsingham, her thoughts

reverting to the wounded men. "Do you allow any visitors, General?"

"There have been some permits given, I believe, to some of the ladies of Trenton, but not many. My staff-surgeon is one of the most particular men in the world, and in matters over which he has any jurisdiction, I assure you I am willing he should take the whole responsibility. He's an excellent man, but an old Betty of a doctor, as I frequently tell him. Still, if you have any desire to see the hospital, I could easily manage it for you."

"I have a little friend," said Lady Walsingham, with great delicacy, "my companion, over there—Molly, you heard what the General said?"

Molly's cheeks were covered with blushes. She arose, after the manner of those primitive times, and gave a demure little curtsey.

"She has a great desire to see an hospital," said Lady Walsingham, after she had sent Molly out on some pretence, "and I have a cupboard stocked with jellies, which I should be glad to dispense—so you will be doing a double favour."

"I shall be very happy," said the General, bowing low. "The little girl has, no doubt, a lover, about whom she is anxious."

"Oh! no—indeed, no;" replied Lady Walsingham, quickly. "I am very sure, from what I know of her father's character, that would never be allowed. Besides, though yesterday she was a provoking little rebel, to-day she shows signs of common-sense, and really, by means of my poor teaching, I hope, begins to betray some interest in our cause."

"I wish, Lady Walsingham, your peculiar means of

conversion could be used in one or two cases of which I have heard. We have some bitter opponents in the youth and beauty of Trenton."

"Indeed, you say truly, General," said Lady Walsingham, her cheeks taking a deeper tinge. "I myself have a niece with whom it is next to impossible to live, so bitter and uncompromising a patriot is she. You may have met her—Miss Elsie Vernon."

"I am happy to say that I have been honoured with some slight tokens of her friendship," said the General, looking down—and no one would have noticed the pain in his voice. "As you say, I should judge her to be unrelenting in her antipathy to the cause of the King."

"Indeed, she is. She and I have had some hot disputes, though I am usually one of the too forbearing kind. But, really, Elsie is intolerable. I charged her once with having a rebel lover," added Lady Walsingham, laughingly.

"And what did she say?" queried the General, with suppressed eagerness.

"Oh! she turned it off as such a very haughty creature might; for, General, she is intensely proud. But, then, of course, I don't believe it myself; I only did it to annoy her, if I must confess as much. You have no idea how many quarrels we have had. We are scarcely on speaking terms, though she's the dearest creature alive, aside from that."

"She is very beautiful," remarked the General, an appearance of relief in his fine features.

"She is, indeed, General," said Lady Walsingham, heartily. "I must declare what one woman seldom does of another, you know—that she is the loveliest girl I ever saw in my life, if she is my niece."

"She does not reside with you, then?"

"Bless me! no," returned the lady; "we couldn't assimilate any easier than oil and water. Neither would she stay with her brother-in-law, who has no mercy in his composition. She is at present with her father's brother, a lawyer; but I question if she will remain with him long. It is an infatuation. She speaks and acts like an inspired creature, and declares that she would lead an army herself if she might but be accepted. She is very bitter against his Majesty, and ridicules the nobility and the Court. Oh! I assure you she is quite noted. The people here worship her, and I really think she would make a very creditable Joan of Arc, if she had the opportunity.

The General arose to go.

"Notwithstanding all this, General, she's a dear, good, generous girl—the daughter of my favourite brother. I hope my tongue has not run away with my judgment."

"I assure you, madam," said the General, with a look that to her seemed one of admiration, "I honour your niece's adherence to what she considers her convictions of duty."

"And shall my little Molly have a pass?"

"It will afford me the greatest pleasure, Lady Walsingham. I will send it by one of my aides."

The General had scarcely gone when letters came. One of these Lady Walsingham opened as soon as she re-entered her room.

"Mercy Molly! come here."

Molly came.

"That wilful girl refuses my overtures."

"Indeed, my lady!"

"And what am I to do without her, I should like to

know? Perhaps she don't think that I need her as much for her suggestions as anything—her taste is exquisite. I don't know what I shall do without her—I don't, indeed! She is excessively provoking."

"I am very sorry," said Molly, humbly, though in her heart she worshipped Miss Elsie, and thought her like the King, who could do no wrong.

"But, Molly, she must come! I can't do without her," cried Lady Walsingham, in real distress.

"Then I'm sure I wish she might come," said Molly.

"Molly, you must go there—you must, child, and use all your powers of persuasion. Picture me entirely helpless without her. I'll excuse her willingly on the night of the party, but she surely must help me with her taste and her fingers. I'm certain I shall never forgive her if she don't!"

"I'll do anything of the kind you wish," said Molly. "Couldn't I go there and to the hospital all under one?"

"No, my dear; the pass may not come in time. It is best that you set off at once for my niece. You will find her—but you know very well where she is stopping."

"At Lawyer William Asbury's, in the red house."

"That's the place. Now, hurry, there's a darling."

CHAPTER IV

THE MAN OF LAW.

THE red house, *par excellence*, was rather an imposing feature at that time. It occupied a conspicuous position, and was approached by several terraces, each reached by a long flight of steps.

Lawyer Asbury, as he was called, was one of the wealthiest men in Trenton. His practice was large, and he had married a fortune—a weak but beautiful woman. Asbury was a man of splendid and extravagant taste. His grounds were laid out with great beauty, and his extreme fear was that there might some time be a battle in Trenton which would disfigure his garden. He was a tall man—quite handsome and dignified, and a violent Tory—so violent that he was often sneered at by his partizans for not taking command of a company himself.

The whole town was astir with the noise and news of the skirmish, which was magnified into a battle. General Washington was reported captured and a great part of his army killed by the Hessians. All the lawyer's family were joyful over the event on the morning after the attack—all but one beautiful girl, whose large, dark eyes were tearless, and her cheeks white as death.

The man of law came in, jubilantly, as the family were about seating themselves at breakfast.

"Great doings!" he cried, "though not so glorious as we anticipated. It was only a skirmish. The ragged vermin expected reinforcements, but they never came; and they were easily despatched, horse and dragoons. It was only a barelegged platoon, any way," he added, laughing.

Elsie glanced up at once. The anger in her eye was at a white heat, and he knew it.

"Remember, Uncle Asbury, those men you speak of are my countrymen," she said severely.

"With all due deference," he answered, with a sarcastic bow, "Miss Vernon may claim them as her relatives, if she pleases."

"I had rather they were than some who are," she answered, with spirit.

"Thank you, Miss Vernon, for the compliment!" he

returned, with blazing eyes. "Your discrimination does you honour. I saw several of these gallant countrymen of yours, and, before heaven, my eyes never beheld such another set of tatterdemalions. There wasn't a whole coat among them, nor a pair of good breeches. A splendid Continental Army, sans shoes, sans stockings, sans everything!"

"Everything except the will and the power to drive these Hessian and British intruders out of the country, and that they will do, mark me, sir, no matter what defeat precedes it. Then, I wonder, who will sneer?"

"When that time comes, Miss Vernon, I promise you to throw up my cap for Washington."

"I accept the promise, and shall hold you to it," said Elsie, rising from the table.

"Very well, Miss Vernon; and now you will, perhaps, condescend to breakfast with us. Perhaps I have more news for you."

"Uncle Asbury, I will never taste food or drink in this house again, till the enemies of my country are driven out of Trenton."

She stood before them all, unwavering—her beautiful eyes soft and steady in their glances, as they encountered the frowning eyes of her uncle.

"Then, my dear, your rash resolve will exclude you for ever, I am very much afraid. You had better think again before you leave us. Your brother-in-law has closed his doors against you, because—"

"It is untrue, sir," cried Elsie, her eyes blazing at the charge. "I left him because I considered him a traitor to his country—in fine, for the same reason that I leave you. I am independent, thank God, and do not need to cringe for favour to anyone whose principles I despise."

"Impertinence!" lisped Mrs. Asbury, who had sat all this time pulling her straw-coloured ringlets. "William, I wonder you don't box her ears."

"I should like to see him or you attempt it," cried Elsie, whose wrath was now intense. "I am only too sorry that I ever condescended to accept the hospitality of this house. And now, uncle, I prophecy," she continued, turning her beautiful face, white and gleaming, toward him, "that before the month is through, your detestable Hessians will be routed and scattered to the four winds by the army of George Washington; and then I shall expect you to lift your cap to the victorious General."

Having said these words, the brave girl left the room.

"I'll not tell her the rest," said the lawyer; "she may find it out as she can."

"Why, what is it?" queried his wife.

"They have captured something more than a tatterdemalion rebel—no other than Lieutenant-Colonel Washburn. He is at present a prisoner, and will, perhaps, turn out a spy. If so, there's the hangman's rope for him."

Elsie stood just within the door. She had heard the last of this cruel speech, and at once comprehended the whole. She could scarcely have turned paler than she did; for one moment her strength seemed to fail her, and she caught at the door. It would not do, however, to let the family behold her emotion; so, resolutely suppressing every trace of suffering, she appeared before them, merely to bid them adieu.

"Ah! so you're really in earnest!" sneered her uncle.

"I thought you knew me by this time," was her calm reply.

"I do know you for a very obstinate young lady," was his answer.

"I shall stop for the present with the widow Green," was the only answer. "If I am inquired for, will you be kind enough to remember?"

"With all the pleasure in the world," said the lawyer. "If any of your barefoot rapscallions among the butchers and shoemakers of Trenton should call upon your ladyship, I will send them to the widow Green, seamstress and laundress *par excellence*—American head-quarters. I have the honour to wish you a very good-morning."

To this insulting speech Elsie replied nothing, but turned away abruptly and left the house.

CHAPTER V

THE PEDLER.

MOLLY trudged along, delighted with the thought that she should soon meet with one with whom she could converse without reserve. The day was fine, clear, and cold. She had nearly reached the little bridge that separated the town, when a party of Hessian soldiers came along. They had been drinking, and were very merry, singing German songs.

Molly looked about her in alarm. There was a small house, not far off, where, in better times, beer and cakes had been sold, but now it seemed quite deserted. The Hessians advanced, and as they came, appeared as if, in a body, they would run her down and crush her. She stood aside, her cheeks flushed, but her heart beating wildly. She was a brave girl, but the sight of twenty or thirty armed foreigners, some of them intoxicated, and flushed with wine and their small victory, made her quail. As they came near, their pace suddenly slackened, and one spoke to another with rude and boisterous laughter.

Molly grew sick and cold. What if they should kill her from mere wantonness, and throw her into the river? There was no chance of escape. Once she was tempted to turn and run, but the act seemed so contemptible to her high spirit, that she almost preferred death.

Suddenly the door of the house that had seemed quite deserted opened, and a little old man, somewhat bent, came out with a small pack on his back. Molly was scarcely breathing now, between her terror and suspense.

The pedler, if that was his calling, walked straight on toward the Hessians, not appearing to notice the trembling girl in the least.

"Ah! fellow-comrades, I have pipes, I have trinkets," he said in German. "I have articles very cheap. Come you this way, and you shall have them for next to nothing."

The men, attracted by the novelty, soon crowded about the pedler, apparently forgetting the frightened Molly, who took advantage of the highway, and walked quickly on, only quickening her pace. After some moments, hearing footsteps, she looked around. The pedler was hastening after her.

"Oh! I thank you so much, my good friend," said Molly, her cheeks now quite blanched.

"It is of no consequence," the man returned in broken English; "I shall see you along a little further. It is imprudent for you to be out alone. Your business must be of importance."

She glanced at him keenly as he said this, but his face was turned away.

"Perhaps it is, and perhaps not," she replied, laughing. "If you were a spy you could get nothing from me."

"But if I were a spy on the right side?"

"Oh! but I should want to see your credentials first."

"Very right. Then, my good girl, look at this when you get home," and he placed a paper in her hand.

She glanced at it and gave a stifled cry.

"Well, what's the matter?"

She looked at him, then at the bold handwriting on the back of the letter before her, so unlike any other that she had ever seen.

"That must be the signature of Captain Paul—"

"Hist!" cried the pedler, as they drew near a knot of people.

"But it is his," she repeated, in a low tone. "Do you know him?" she added, eagerly; "is he alive?"

"He was, last night," was the low response.

"Great heaven! is he here?"

"Here! Why, little woman, do you know how many miles a man can travel between sunset and sunrise?"

"Oh! then you saw him somewhere—he is not dead?" and her cheek flushed again.

"He is not dead, to my certain knowledge," was the reply.

Molly looked down, but said nothing. Again her heart was beating almost fiercely, but not with dread. All doubt was at an end. She had no motive now for visiting the little hospital. Paul Green, her handsome lover, was yet living. The stranger watched her furtively. He saw the eyes grow bright and sparkling—noted the quick movement of her bodice—her abstracted manner—and said to himself:

"She loves him—she loves him!"

"Oh! here I am, at Lawyer Asbury's," cried Molly, looking up from her delicious reverie. "Thank you a thousand times for your kindness and protection, and if you should need any advice, call at Lady Walsingham's—you will be sure to find me."

"A noted Tory house, eh?"

"True, but she is a kind, good woman, and does not feel as even some of those who were born in this country. As for me, I have no choice—my father put me there."

"And your father is a Tory, though you are not, I take it."

"You have no right to question me," was the quick reply.

"True. I beg your pardon," and the queer old man passed on.

"Great heaven! what have I said?" cried Molly to herself. "The man may be a spy, and I never thought"—and she reviewed his questions and her answers.

"I think I was careful," she mumured, as she went slowly from terrace to terrace. "As for this letter, whatever it is, I'll read it and burn it."

"Little Molly Putnam, from Lady Walsingham's," echoed Mrs. Asbury. "Let her come in. No doubt she has brought me a note for the great party."

"Well, my dear," cried the lawyer's wife, "and how is my Lady Walsingham?"

"Yes, how is my dear, my precious Lady Walsingham?" whistled a small, affected voice, and Molly, glancing up, saw the most grotesque miniature of a woman that she had ever met in her life, painted and padded and patched and powdered, and so altogether made up, that it was difficult to tell where any part of the real woman was.

"This is Miss Lydia Lavoy, my dear, who used to be such a famous belle. No doubt, you have heard of her."

"Used to be the toast of all the young gentlemen, my dear," put in the other, complacently smoothing out the folds of her sea-green silk, "and not bad looking now, considering she has passed her thirtieth year. Do you think so?"

Molly could hardly keep from laughing outright, as the antiquated little woman, who had probably seen her sixtieth winter, bobbed down upon the sofa. But, she had no time to spend in compliments.

"I came to see Miss Elsie, on her aunty's account," she said, turning to the lawyer's wife.

"Then, my dear, you must go to a very low and common place to find her," replied Mrs. Asbury. Molly opened her eyes, quite terrified.

"Yes, Miss Vernon took offence at something her Uncle Charles said about the ragged troops of General Washington, and chose to leave our protection. I think she lives with that old laundress in the lane. You know her, a Mrs. Green, I think."

Molly's cheek burned as if she had been insulted; but remembering the *rôle* she had proposed to herself to play, she suppressed the indignation trembling on her lips.

"I hardly think Mrs. Green should be called a laundress," she replied, as respectfully as she could, "because when the American officers wanted their linen done up she volunteered to have it washed. You know, Mrs. Asbury, there were so many Tories in town that the washerwomen were all afraid to work for the Continental army. I am sure Mrs. Green has always been a lady."

"The kind of lady that I have no wish to associate with," said Mrs. Asbury, with a sneer. "However, lady or no lady, Miss Vernon has seen fit to make her home with her."

Away turned Molly, freighted with compliments from poor Miss Lydia Lavoy to Walsingham House. She took her way to the pleasant lane on the outskirts, where widow Green resided, in a quaint, picturesque, two-storied cottage.

CHAPTER VI.
TWO DISCOVERIES.

A MAN, old in figure, leaned over the little oaken table pointing out the outlines of a map. His face was hidden by luxuriant curls, which it was the fashion for the men of that day to wear.

The room was an apartment—the widow Green's cottage—a large, sunny, homely parlour, which, apart from a few good pictures, and two or three elegant pieces of antique furniture, had in it nothing unusual. An old eight-day clock ticked in the corner, its tall mahogany frame looking gaunt and care-worn with time, for it was a heir-loom, and very ancient. A yellow painted spinning-wheel could be seen through the open door that led into the kitchen.

On the opposite side of the table stood Elsie Vernon, her beautiful face quite colourless, and though she was listening attentively, seeming to regard the proceedings before her with far-away glances. Next to her, her whole attention absorbed, the widow Green leaned partly on her son's shoulder, as she watched the intricacies of the map.

Outside, near the gate, stood uncouth Hannah, the only serving-maid and faithful friend and attendant of the widow through many years, both of prosperity and adversity. She was to wave or lift a red handkerchief carelessly, if she saw anyone coming.

"There you see," said the pedler, still intent upon his explanations, "how it was the General feared the enemy might pass behind him. There is Northcastle, and here is where he fortified. He always gives his soldiers something to protect them, if it is possible. Why, I've known him to throw up a barrier in twelve hours that looked as though a thousand forty-pounders couldn't breach it, and yet, I suppose well-planted cannon could have knocked it to flinders. He's great for strategy, is General Washington. Lee has a splendid reputation in the army, but, with all his military acumen, he was surprised and captured at a little farm-house off here."

"So that story was true!" said Elsie. "I was so mortified when my uncle told me."

"The whole army was mortified," returned the young man. "They'll never catch Washington napping in that way. You see Fort Lee; it is on the west bank of the Hudson, opposite Fort Washington. Well, there was where we made our retreat. It was a dark time, I assure you, with a great well-disciplined army in our rear. We lost almost everything — tents, baggage, artillery, and provisions. But, by heavens! nothing discourages the General. No matter how much the men complain, or the officers grumble. By the way—"

"See, Mrs. Green, Hannah has the handkerchief flying," cried Elsie.

Up went the battered hat of the pedler—in which the thick dark locks were hidden, and the face assumed its old grim expression.

"Oh! it's only Molly, the dear little thing," cried Elsie, again going to the window. "Captain Paul, I don't think you need be afraid of her."

"I don't, indeed," replied the other, who had hastily drawn out his small pack, and thrust the crumpled map into his pocket, while, through the psuedo wrinkles on his face, the blood leaped redly. "Still, it may be best to be cautious," he added, with a smile.

"Molly, darling!" cried Elsie, with whom the young girl was a great favourite.

"Oh! Miss Elsie, I'm so glad!" She turned and started with astonishment. "Why! here's the pedler, who protected me so kindly on the road."

"Protected you?" echoed Elsie and the widow.

"Should you know him again?" asked a well-remembered voice, that set all her pulses beating, and the pedler lifted the battered old cap, showing a fine breadth of forehead and his luxuriant hair.

"Remember—oh! Captain Paul!" cried Molly, her cheeks covered with blushes. He held up his finger; Molly's eyes fell. To think he should have deceived her so! Again she tried to recollect all she had said to him. Did he notice her delight when she recognized his handwriting? Not only her cheeks but her ears tingled now. In her confusion she felt as if she should sink through the floor. Elsie noticed her agitation and quickly divined the cause.

"Come with me, Molly," she said; "I have something to tell you."

"Oh! Miss Elsie, would you have dreamed it was Captain Paul?" cried Molly, when they were alone together."

"No, my dear, we neither of us recognized him—not

even his mother. Why, my child, the tears are in your eyes!"

"I—I feel wretchedly nervous," half sobbed Molly.

"Indeed, my poor little girl, we have all cause to feel wretchedly nervous. You did not hear, perhaps, that Lieutenant-Colonel Washburn was a prisoner?"

"Oh! Miss Elsie!" cried Molly, forgetting all her troubles, "that can't be possible."

"I fear it is, though it may have been an invention of my uncle, to disconcert and trouble me."

"That splendid young gentleman," cried Molly. "Is he in the custody of the Hessian General, do you think?"

"You mean General Rahl? He must be, my dear, of course, if he is a prisoner. The last time I heard of him he was at Fort Washington. How he came here I cannot tell."

"General Rahl was at your aunt's but this morning."

"Is that so?" queried Elsie, with new interest.

"Yes; he is to be present at a grand party to be given at Walsingham House on Christmas night. It was to beg you to go there, on or before the occasion, that Lady Walsingham sent me here.

"She knows I would not," cried Elsie, indignantly.

"She says she can never get along without your taste and skill. She intends to make a great many decorations," said Molly.

"Oh, yes! she wishes to use me—I see," cried Elsie, remembering their last interview, and her aunt's cool insolence.

"But, Miss Elsie, pardon me :—I have been thinking it would be better to be on good terms with these people."

"The enemies of our country! This from you, Molly Putnam!" cried Elsie, with real anger.

"I would not have dared to say as much yesterday, even to myself."

"But what has changed your mind?"

"The fear that—that—" Molly looked down distressed. "I may as well make a clean breast of it," she added, looking up and smiling through her tears, "the fear that some one I loved might be in peril. I even was bold enough to beg for a pass from the General, to visit the hospital."

"Admirable, Molly!" cried Elsie, her eyes kindling with enthusiasm. "I see your drift. Is it possible that you can really get into the hospital—perhaps go through the camp of the Hessians?"

"Is it not worth trying?"

"Yes, yes—anything," cried Elsie, breathlessly, below her voice. "Yes, yes, I comprehend—you are a better strategist than I am, Molly. Tell my aunt she may expect me on the 23rd, and that I shall be happy to do everything in my power. Indeed, I will please her; and, Molly, think what a great thing it would be to liberate him."

"Oh! indeed, Miss Elsie, if we could do that, you and I would be heroines for life. How shall we manage it?"

"I wonder if it would please my aunt if I came directly?" mused Elsie.

"I think she would be delighted," Molly made answer.

"Then I'll do it. Molly, you must use your permit."

"This very afternoon!" echoed Molly.

"And then—you do not know him, though?"

"I not know Lieutenant-Colonel Washburn? Have I not seen him at Walsingham House at least twice?"

"True enough; I had forgotten. Well, I trust to your woman's wit to find him."

"I'll do it, or my name's not Molly."

"Good little Molly! Let us seal our compact with a kiss. There! now it is settled."

"Yes, I'm to be a heroine, if I die for it," laughed Molly.

"Find out for me, Molly, if my aunt really desires me to come, and send word by somebody at the house."

"Yes; and, Miss Elsie, trust me but what I'll get you some word from him. I've wit enough for that, at all events."

"A thousand thanks, darling, till you can be better repaid. And now we'll go down and see the old pedler."

"Is he a spy?" asked Molly, fearfully.

"Whatever he is, my dear, he has the good of our country at heart," returned Elsie, gravely.

"But, oh! Miss Elsie, if he is suspected, he will be hung."

"Don't let that thought enter your mind again," returned Elsie. "With that make-up, I don't think any one could possibly suspect him; besides, he has so much tact and wisdom. Even his mother did not recognize him, and I find it difficult, when he is disguised, to believe that it is Captain Paul. At this crisis, my dear, men must not shirk peril. Which had you rather lose, your lover or your country?"

"God help me to say—my lover," responded Molly, solemnly.

"Amen to that!" cried Elsie, with closed eyes, but when she opened them, tears stood on the beautiful lashes.

At that moment a familiar voice sounded from the wood. Both girls ran to the window. It was old Glan Ratcliffe, as he was called by the loyalists, talking to somebody across the road.

"A spy! did you say?" cried the opposite voice.

"That's what they say now," replied Ratcliffe—"papers found upon him that'll hang him. Serves him right for a fool. I always said Harry Washburn would come to a bad end."

Elsie withdrew her face. Death would not have altered it. The two girls looked in one another's faces; Molly burst into tears.

"Hush, Molly; don't you see how calm I am?" said Elsie. And, indeed, the quiet of her voice and manner was something fearful.

"Oh! Miss Elsie—it would kill you," sobbed Molly.

"I'm not sure but it would," replied Elsie, with that same far-off look in her eyes; "but, now, we must redouble our exertions; we must move heaven and earth but what we release him."

"Yes," she murmured, "yes, I would even do that, to save a life so valuable to his country. My God! be Thou the friend of the friendless now!"

"Molly," she continued, "not a word about this to any one, not even to Captain Paul. What is said to him I will say myself."

Molly promised silence, and, after a few moments, the two girls went down-stairs together.

Paul would not let Molly go alone. There were squads of drunken soldiers all over the town, he said; and, though he did not walk with her, he was still near enough to keep her in view till she reached Walsingham House in safety.

CHAPTER VII.

THE NIGHT AT VALLEY FORGE.

THE wind whistled along the gloomy banks of the Delaware river, and seemed to moan with ever-increasing violence at that part where Washington's troops were encamped. Here and there guards were stationed, but the freezing air penetrated the worn-out clothing of the soldiers, and their feet, frost-bitten and often bleeding from the want of sufficient protection, left, in some places, the traces of their suffering.

Washington sat in a large unfurnished room of a deserted farm-house. Beside him stood an oaken table, covered with paper. In the great chimney-place a huge fire roared; but he did not seem to be thinking of the warmth. Indeed, the rattling of the windows was simultaneous with the heavy, sweeping draughts that seemed to penetrate every nook and corner; to protect himself from which, Washington had thrown an old army coat over his shoulders.

At that period the Continental leader was nearer discouragement than, perhaps, ever before or after. The men were, many of them, dissatisfied and grumbling. They were short of rations, short of clothes, and closely under the surveillance of a large Royalist army. A large body of the people could not sympathise with him, so greatly were they influenced by the Tories. It was a dark hour, as may be seen by the following extracts from a letter lying at that moment unfolded. The pen with which it was written stood on the rude rack, still glistening with ink :—

"If every nerve is not strained to recruit the army, I think the game is pretty nearly up. You can form no idea of the perplexity of my situation. No man, I believe, ever had a greater choice of evils, and less means to extricate himself from them."

In one corner of the room, a sort of "shake-down" had been made, and a soldier was lying there under his cloak. It was one of the General's aides, a Captain Cuyler. Nearer the fire, his chair tilted back, his arms folded, his brows contracted, sat another officer, a Colonel Rest.

The two candles, one on the high, narrow shelf, the other on the table, only added to the general gloom.

Suddenly Washington roused himself from his reverie.

"It's a terrible night," he said.

"Terrible, indeed. Ice is making fast in the river. I wonder when it will bear the weight of an army?"

Washington smiled gloomily.

"I don't think we shall stay for that," he replied.

"Cornwallis is not thirty miles off, they say," replied the colonel.

"I don't doubt it," Washington responded. "I only wish we were the pursuing party, and the river before them."

"Confound him!" muttered the colonel, still referring to Cornwallis. "It is in vain to look for reinforcements; the people will give us no help."

"But they will throw up their hats if we whip the Hessians," said Washington, grimly. "Here is Lee a prisoner, and Reed a traitor, at least to me; while the subordinate officers are quarrelling about promotion."

"We shall look back to these dark days, General, with a little pardonable pride."

"Yes, sir, we shall;" cried General Washington, as if nerved with a fresh idea. "I trust in God we shall. At all events, nothing shall be wanting on my part, in the midst of every discouragement; and we have discouragements enough, God knows. The enemy must be in total ignorance of our numbers and situation, or they would never suffer us to remain unmolested. Sir William Howe is expected, and Cornwallis is close upon us. Our prisoners are suffering and languishing; everything looks dark, I admit, yet give me but a few trusty friends, and I promise victory. Yes, victory; I feel it in every fibre of my frame."

"Your words are inspiriting, General."

The door opened; one of the guards appeared. The General motioned him to the fire, for it had begun to rain, and every part of the poor fellow's ragged uniform was dripping.

"I am sorry it is so bad a night," said the General. "Well, you have some intelligence."

"A stranger has arrived, with letters and credentials, who insists upon seeing the General," said the soldier. "He is a foreigner."

General Washington held a short conference with the colonel, then ordered that the stranger be admitted. He stood before him soon, a small, dark, keen-eyed Polish officer. The General read his letter of introduction from Dr. Franklin.

"Sir, you come to us in the darkest time of our history," said Washington. "What do you seek here?"

The stranger drew up his form with a gesture of pride.

"I come here to fight for American independence," he said.

Washington smiled. The straightforward answer pleased him.

"But, what can you do?"

"Try me," was the quiet reply.

"With pleasure," returned the General; and, calling a servant, he sent him up-stairs to assign quarters to Kosciusko.

The storm grew yet fiercer. Gusts of snow and rain swept against the windows; without was darkness and cold; the almost freezing soldiers tried in vain to coax warmth into ragged blankets; many of the tents were displaced, and the sentinels had all they could do to keep life in their stiffening limbs.

It was twelve o'clock by the old kitchen time-piece when Washington laid down his pen and proposed to retire. The servant came in and heaped more wood on the fire. Then he brought a couple of blankets and something that looked like a pillow, and placed them near the hearth, for Washington sometimes slept Indian fashion, his feet toward the fire. It was a ghostly night; unearthly voices sounded at intervals when the loose blocks of ice in the Delaware came together with a crash. The Delaware! so soon to bear on its bosom a freight precious to freedom and history!

CHAPTER VIII.

LIFE OR DEATH.

ONLY the breathing of the sleepers could be heard within; only the tread of the sentinel at times, as the wind brought in the noise from without.

Suddenly, in the distance, came the regular tramp of horses' feet. The soldiers listened, portending evil, but before long the sentinels were relieved by the low spoken talismanic word, which proved that the man before them, wet and haggard, was one of themselves. His business, he said, admitted of no delay—he must see General Washington.

At the approach of this horseman, another than the soldiers and sentinels outside had apprehended danger. Some time after Washington had thrown himself down, this man had half-risen, warily, and peered out into the now brightly illuminated room. A haggard, remorseful expression marked his face, though he was young and handsome. His lips were closely pressed together—his eyes were gleaming and desperate. At one moment it seemed as if he were about to rise, and the soldier on guard at the door, turned his sleepy vision in that direction. The captain thought better, however, and by the time the midnight intruder made his appearance before Washington, he feigned a sound sleep.

Washington was a light sleeper. As he stood up to receive the new-comer, he looked as fresh as if he had rested for a night.

"I am Captain Green, of the 10th New Jersey Volunteers," said the young officer, with a respectful salute. "Since noon to-day I have ridden from Trenton."

Washington's eye lighted.

"The Hessians are there in considerable force, commanded by General Rahl," continued the young man. "On the 19th, three regiments stationed near the town, received false news that reinforcements were expected. The communication was regarded as coming from yourself, and, with high hopes, they engaged a party of Hessians, thinking they were isolated from the main body. I regret to say that it ended disastrously to our small army, and the Hessians completely routed the volunteers, killing some, wounding many, and taking one prisoner of rank—Lieutenant-Colonel Washburn."

Washington's brow clouded.

There was a quick movement opposite. Captain Cuyler moved uneasily, muttering as if in sleep.

"But worse than this, by some papers found upon his person, he is condemned as a spy, and will be hung on the 28th—the day after Christmas."

"My brave young friend!" cried the General, in a suppressed voice. "We must not allow this—murder—for it is nothing less. Washburn was no spy."

"We are all ready to stake our lives on his innocence. I have taken advantage of the peculiar state of things," continued Captain Green, with a significant smile, "and here is the result of my inquiries."

He laid notes, and a small map, rudely outlined in pencil, before Washington.

"Thanks, my brave comrade," said Washington; "if his service affects us favourably, your promotion is sure;" and seating himself, he called the colonel to his side. The three sat there for an hour, and at the end of that time Washington said:—

"The blow must be struck then or never. We must effect the crossing at Christmas. It will never do to let those foreign rascals murder that honourable soldier. Remember that, for the time being, we are sworn to secrecy."

"How do you propose to cross, General?" queried the colonel.

"In boats."

"Will it be possible?"

"It must be."

"We have some splendid sailors," said the colonel.

"Yes, the Marblehead regiment."

An hour after this, complete silence reigned once more in the old farm-house.

The fire had burned low, casting now and then fitful flashes through the gloom. Washington slept soundly; so, apparently, did all but the one man on guard, who had much ado to keep his eyes open.

Presently the captain upon the shakedown lifted his head.

"Donelly," he whispered.

The man's hand went to his slouched cap.

"There's a bottle of whisky in the cupboard, and a drinking horn. Bring them here, will you? I feel ill."

"Sart'in, sir," said the man, with another salute, and he went softly for the coveted articles—his eyes now quite bright and wide awake.

"Will you take some, Donelly? It will keep you warm."

"Will I? Sure, you know I'll consider it a blessin' this night."

"Well, here—one horn will do you no harm; quick, man," and he poured out a large quantity, which Donelly drank, ending with a satisfied smack, and crept back to his place.

"If worse comes to worst," muttered the young man, in an undertone, "they'll say he had a fit—or that it was him who tried it—or—great God! what a night it is!" and he pretended to drink some of the whisky, his hand shaking like that of a guilty coward all the while.

The hours passed on, and the only seemingly living thing in that room were the captain's eyes, that now and then glared fearfully. The poor sentinel, under the influence of a powerful drug, lay crouched up against the door. Washington's face and head were bare, and somehow the thin flame that now and then lifted itself up makily from the half-spent embers, fell upon his noble face—the grand brow from which the thick hair swept naturally; the calm greatness of the man's countenance was most impressive in this awful period.

For on that hour hung the balance of America's fate as a nation.

Captain Cuyler had become passionately enamoured of a beautiful English girl, at that time residing in New York. The infatuation of her only brother—as she called it—had led him to forsake his family and join the American cause. For this, and for other reasons, her hatred of the Continental army was intense. She had inspired this young American captain with an almost idolatrous love, and after playing fast and loose with him for months, at length consented to reward him with her hand, if ever he succeeded, by fair means or foul, in ridding the country of its great father and patriot—Washington.

Imagine, then, what hellish thoughts must have possessed his mind! How, day after day, he had been nerving himself for this dastardly deed, till his reflections were all of blood—his dreams of murder.

And now the time had come. Treachery was abroad—treachery within. The darkness had an awful meaning to him. Should he bring that upon his soul for which no repentance could possibly atone?

The winds without muttered and moaned. There was a voice in every cadence. Their very whispers were as evil portents to him. Did spirits ride abroad on their fearful pinions? Were there awful, unseen agencies within his very grasp? As the time approached he shook with apprehension. Had remorse seized upon him so soon?

There, at his mercy, lay that august head. There, at the point of his steel, trusting and pure as ever man's purposes could be in any righteous cause, lay that noble heart. Again and again he turned away his head, as that thin, white dagger of flame gleamed upon the features of the commander whom all men loved. Across his memory rushed all the kindly words that he had spoken, all the noble deeds that he had done. Should a woman's smile and a home of grandeur weigh against these?

"My God! how can I!" the young man groaned, in anguish.

"But I cannot lose her," and again the hand of treachery was uplifted.

"I choose between my country and my own selfish love;" not in just those words did the thought come to him; nevertheless it did come. Suddenly one blast, shriller than all the rest, seemed to whistle in his ear the word:—

"Murderer!"

He started back, glaring over his shoulder, thrusting his long dark hair from either ear; his eyes dilated as if with madness. And there came a vision before him, with awful distinctness—the portrait of a memory—a pale, sweet face—pale, sad lips, that called him lovingly—eyes frosted by death, yet beaming tenderness upon her boy—the memory of a dying mother. Quick as thought he sprung to his feet.

"I will not do this deed!" he cried. "I swear by my Maker and my honour, I will not! Better misery—life-long—better death!"

"What is it?" The voice was Washington's, who waked as easily as he slept. "Sentinel, are you there?"

"Here, sir," replied the young captain, who now stood before the sleeping soldier.

"All right!" said Washington, drowsily, and, unconscious of the dreadful tragedy that had been contemplated, he sunk again into slumber.

Rousing himself in the early morning, Washington was surprised to find young Captain Cuyler, who was a favourite of his, standing in place of the sleeping soldier. He was pale and ghostlike, for a night of intense mental suffering had acted fearfully upon his sensitive temperament.

"What does this mean?" asked Washington; "is Donelly dead?"

"Dead tired, General," answered young Cuyler. "I pitied the poor fellow, and took his place."

"You assumed a peculiar responsibility, young sir," replied the General, in a voice which he tried to make stern. "However, it speaks well for the goodness of your heart."

The sleeping sentinel was roused with difficulty, and, half dead with terror, besought the captain to exculpate him, and his tremour was scarcely allayed by the assurance that Washington knew of it, and had forgiven him.

The day had scarcely waned when, among the letters brought to camp, was one by a famous scout, directed to Captain Cuyler. The young man received it with apathy, for the handwriting was not what he expected.

He opened it—then sat glaring, his eyes wide and white with agony.

Miss Letty Washburn was dead!

On the receipt of news that her brother was a prisoner and condemned to death, she had been seized with convulsions, and died almost instantly.

Where now would have been the reward for his treachery? A fugitive and a wanderer had he been this hour—a skulking vagabond; the murderer not only of a man, but of a nation!

No wonder that within twenty-four hours there were silver threads in the dark hair. That baptism of sorrow made him old before his time.

CHAPTER IX.

THE FAIR CONSPIRATORS

To go back and take up the thread, broken for the introduction of this episode.

Molly was received at Walsingham House with rapture.

"So Elsie is coming? I have been fretting over an expected refusal. Why, little Molly, what charm have you? I never dreamed you would succeed."

"I think she wearies of this continued strife with her family," said Molly.

"Poor child! and, after all, she is not so much to blame. Her father brought her up, and all but laid his dying command upon her. I wish she would only be a little more reasonable," said Lady Walsingham.

"She will be, perhaps, after this."

Lady Walsingham could have kissed Molly. The young girl always had been a favourite, and Lady Walsingham, who had been raised to fortune and a title from the ranks of the people by virtue of a pretty face and a wonderful ambition, had no life-long prejudices to sacrifice in making this pretty country maid almost her equal. Besides, old Father Putnam was a rich man, and put his daughter there because, in his foolish old heart, he thought that she might have advantages that would favour the formation of genteel manners. He wanted his girl to be "a lady," he said. So when Lady Walsingham, who had come from England only some two years previous to attend to business affairs, which her husband formerly had managed, saw, and took a violent fancy to sweet Molly Putnam, he consented, at once, that she should take the position offered, though not for wages.

"Now I can make your heart glad," said Lady Walsingham. "Here's a permit for you to visit the hospital. It was brought by a delightful Hessian, who spoke barbarous English, in which, putting together words enough to make a long harangue, I could only distinguish two of them."

Molly's eyes glistened.

"But will you want to go alone, child? I think I had better send Joe with you. He is so silly that nobody will be afraid of him, but he thinks so much of you that he could protect you."

She rung the bell. Another moment, and Joe Stupid, as the servants called him, a half-witted boy, stood upon the threshold.

"Joe," said Lady Walsingham, "you're to go to the hospital with Miss Molly here."

"Won't I though?" was Joe's delighted answer. "Ain't I grateful? Wouldn't I go to Chiny with her? Don't—"

"That will do, Joe. Go and get ready, and be sure you follow her closely, and keep silence."

"Won't I though? Ain't I—"

"There, there, Joe—no talking: hurry, or Miss Molly will go without you."

Joe was soon ready, and following Molly so closely that he seemed to be ambitious to tread in her particular footsteps. The old church stood in a sort of open area. On one side it was quite hemmed in by thickly-set pines; on the other only a wide field bounded the vision.

Molly showed her permit, and was allowed to enter. Both Joe and herself bore baskets, the boy's being one of large dimensions.

The interior of the church had been stripped bare of seats, and rudely-constructed cots and beds laid all around. At first, Molly thought she never could have the courage to enter. The sight of so many pale faces, so many appliances for surgery, so many grave severe-looking officers, particularly the surgeons, who seemed to frown upon her, disconcerted her terribly. However, she mustered up courage at last, and, finding out to whom she might distribute her delicacies, she was soon busy among both friends and foes.

There was not a familiar face among them, and she was not allowed to speak to her own countrymen. How should she get access to the camp, for that was now her solicitude? If she spoke to the officers, they chose not to understand her, and probably they did not, for, among them all, only one might have been taken for an Englishman by the purity of his accent, and that was General Rahl, who was nowhere visible.

Molly prolonged her visit to the hospital as long as she dared. As she left the building, General Rahl was just then dismounting at the door. He recognised Molly at once.

"So you came; and are you satisfied that a hospital is not as pleasant a place as a camp?"

"How can I tell, unless I had seen a camp?" Molly

innocently inquired, and she smiled very pleasantly at the General.

"Would it please you to see a camp?"

"Oh! very much," cried Molly, with enthusiasm.

"Then, if you will wait here one little moment, your servant can hold my horse, and I will myself accompany you."

Fortunate Molly—to have for an escort no less than the great General Rahl! But Molly did not think of the distinction; her soul was engrossed in the plot of which she was continually dreaming. To become a heroine in a good cause was the sole ambition of her life.

Presently the General came out, and they walked along the main road together.

"You are—did I understand—a relation of Lady Walsingham?" he inquired.

"I am a friend of Lady Walsingham's, sir, not a relation."

"Ah! I mistook. Lady Walsingham is a beautiful woman."

"She is indeed, sir, but you should see her niece."

"I have seen Miss Elsie Vernon."

"That is she—the loveliest creature I ever knew."

"Lovely, indeed, but unfortunately our inclinations diverge in such a manner as to render a close acquaintance almost impossible."

"You mean, sir—"

"That she is a rebel."

"Now, I think you are mistaken, General Rahl," said Molly, quietly.

"What! is she not a violent anti-Royalist?"

"Not as violent as she might be. She has modified her opinions somewhat."

"Since when?" and the General looked eagerly in Molly's eyes.

"Since very recently, I may say. The truth is, it is not pleasant, living in a constant broil with members of one's family."

"Indeed, I should think not," murmured the General, absently.

"And she has concluded to live at peace with them."

"A wise conclusion," he answered.

"It may be that she will ignore the Republican cause altogether," said Molly, going in her zeal much further than circumstances warranted, or her friend would have approved.

"I believe I understood that the young lady was residing with Lawyer Asbury, who is her uncle."

"She was there," said Molly, "but she is expected at Walsingham House for a long visit."

A gleam of pleasure crossed the General's face.

"So she will probably grace the entertainment on Christmas night."

"Undoubtedly," said Molly. "I think if she had been there to-day, I might have been tempted to trespass upon your generosity. I know she wishes to see both the camp and the hospital."

"Nothing would delight me more than to show them to her," said the General, with the enthusiasm of a lover. "Will you say so, from me? It will give me the keenest pleasure."

"I will say so, and I am almost certain that she will accept. But oh! here is the camp. Why, it is like a little city!"

"Our military ideas of order are very strict," he said, smiling.

"And pray, have you any prisoners?" she asked, carelessly. "It seems to me I heard of some."

"Only one of any note, and I fear it will shock you to hear that he is under sentence of death."

"Dear, dear! that is terrible," said Molly, with a sudden pallor, that, however, escaped his eye. "Pray, what has he done? I did not know that you always shot your prisoners."

"Neither do we, except in cases like this. If we find a spy, we do not shoot, we hang him."

"Oh! that is more awful still," cried Molly, involuntarily placing her hand to her throat; "you are cruel, you are barbarous."

"So I dare say we seem, but it is not so. It is the rules of war—a spy is hung almost without judge or jury."

"But you could save him."

"Oh! the pardoning power lies with me, of course," said the General, "but I would not exercise it in such a case as that. It would be a dangerous precedent."

Molly was silent for a few moments; something seemed to rise in her throat and choke her.

"Do you hang them right away?" she asked, in a low voice.

"Sometimes—but we have given this young man grace. He will not be executed till the day after Christmas."

Molly's face brightened.

"I'm sure that you can feel no sympathy with the enemies of the King," he said, a moment after.

"Oh! of course not, but it would be so—so interesting to see a prisoner under such circumstances!"

"Why, that is a little bloodthirsty."

"And if Miss Elsie and myself should visit the camp again, I think, I am almost sure, it would afford her pleasure, also."

"To see a man under sentence of death? Well, you shall be gratified if you bring Miss Vernon here, I promise you. But I am afraid it may make you morbidly sensitive. The young man happens to be interesting, and handsome, too."

"Oh! we'll promise to be very proper," replied Molly, with great difficulty concealing a break in her voice. What would she have given could she at that moment have allowed free vent to the tears that were crowding up from her heart.

It was not long before Elsie and she were closeted together, laying plans that were no sooner formed than they seemed impossible to undertake. But they were brave as well as tender spirits—those two gentle girls—and did not despair.

"Even should we see him," said Elsie, "we cannot communicate with him."

"Did you say once that he had a dumb sister?" asked Molly.

"Yes, he has two sisters—the youngest, a child, is dumb."

"Then, of course, he knows the deaf and dumb alphabet."

"Oh, yes! I have often seen him use it."

"And so do I!" cried Molly, joyfully. "My mother could only talk by signs two years before she died, and that compelled her to study it."

"Molly, you are my angel!" said Elsie, fervently. "While the attention of the others is turned another way, you could certainly contrive to say a word or two."

"I am sure I could," said Molly. "Now, suppose it to be one word. What should you choose?"

"Hope," said Elsie.

"And look—it is said," laughed Molly. "We shall save him!"

CHAPTER X.

PEDDLING TO SOME PURPOSE.

THE prisoner had, meantime, abandoned the delicious feeling portrayed by that word, hope. He felt that his doom was drawing near.

He had been placed in a small house on the outskirts of the camp, under a strong guard, and there passed his solitary hours. It was hard to stare death in the face thus, and he so young; hard to feel that liberty not only, but life were denied him. And he was innocent—not of the charge of fighting against the King, but of being a spy. Unfortunately he had accepted the effects of a brother officer, who had gained some special information of the enemy's whereabouts, and these were found upon him. He had not thought of them until they were discovered, and then whatever explanations he made were disbelieved, so he maintained a haughty silence.

His room was very small, the windows overlooking the camp, so that he wearied of the scene. His thoughts turned backward. He had voluntarily deserted his family for the sake of the cause for which he was to die ignominiously. His proud sister, he knew, considered that he disgraced them all. Yet he was sure that if she heard of his present situation, it would nearly, if not quite, cause her death.

Yes, the past was continually before him. He had

become acquainted with Elsie Vernon, only to love her with the fondest and purest affection; and now, almost within sight of the house where he had first seen her, he should die a disgraceful death.

How the hot blood dyed his forehead as he went over the imagined preliminaries in the horrible scene! And yet his heart swelled with a human sorrow that he should never again, perhaps, see the woman of his love. He had heard some vague hints relative to General Rahl's admiration of the beautiful Miss Vernon, but he knew her too well to suppose that she reciprocated the least favour.

"It would be pleasanter to die in my bed," he murmured, looking toward the burning west; "it would be glorious to fall in battle; but to be strung up like a common criminal—that is too terrible, and for a crime of which I am not guilty."

As he was saying this, little Molly was just parting from the commander outside the entrance of the camp.

Presently he heard voices.

"It's that little Dutch pedler, again," said one of his guards. "He has some very nice things, and very cheap. I shouldn't wonder—" and he made a motion as if in the act of drinking.

"Why can't he come in?" asked the elder and stouter man.

"Against orders," was the reply.

"Nonsense! He's only a pedler, well known about here, I presume, and a furious Royalist."

"How do you know?"

"We met him, this morning, a party of us, and he talked just right. It it wasn't for a lame arm, he says, he should be with us, but that makes it impossible."

"Oh! let him come in," exclaimed the other. "We want something to break the monotony of this place. There's no danger to apprehend."

The young officer, who stood moodily gazing from the window, knew enough of German to make out that they were interested in the pedler, and he could not help turning as the man came in. It was a careless scrutiny, however—he had never seen the man before, but the change was a relief. He was tired of the two burly guards.

The pack was set upon the floor; the pedler looked warily round; his eye caught that of the lieutenant-colonel, but it was stolid and dull as ever.

Presently he opened his budget, displaying trinkets of all sorts. Red silk handkerchiefs lay in fine contrast to white clay pipes. Meantime he rattled on in German, praising the beauty of his wares, offering them at a price almost next to nothing, and that must have been considerably below the cost of even very inferior articles.

Among other things was a showy pocketbook, with silver clasps, which took the fancy of the elder Hessian.

"That's a beautiful thing," said the pedler, in German, "and so cheap. You mark that inscription there; and the crimson edges match your top-boots. See!" and he held them against those appendages.

The Germans gravely inspected it.

"What does it say?" asked the younger one.

"Ah! you would be glad to know. But, perhaps, you want me to think you don't know English," he said, his countenance changing.

They protested, each of them, that they did not understand one word of the language.

By this time the prisoner was quite interested, in spite

of his apathy, and was even straining his eyes to make out, if possible, what was written upon the pocketbook.

"Then first I will read it in English," said the pedler, "and afterward translate it; what say you?"

"Agreed!" was the answer.

The pedler lifted himself, stood with his back to the window, so that the light fell on the pocketbook, and enunciated, softly and distinctly:—

"I am Captain Paul Green, of the 10th New Jersey Volunteers. Having heard that my superior officer was in danger of his life from a false charge, I decided to leave Trenton to-night for Washington's camp, and find some means, if possible, to liberate him."

It was well that young Washburn stood partly in the shade, for the strong emotion that almost shook his frame—the thing coming so unexpectedly upon him—changed his face to a death-like pallor. Then rose a flush of deepest joy and gratitude; he leaned heavily against the wall, for his strength seemed to have deserted him.

"Well, boys, now do you want the inscription in Hessian?" cried the pedler, turning a comical glance toward them, never having trusted himself to look at the prisoner.

They both assented, and the pedler continued:—

"This pocketbook has a charm imparted by the seventh son of a seventh son, and will never be empty while the first purchaser carries it, if it be for forty years."

"You see it contains already a small sum of money," he said, opening one of the pockets and displaying a German copper coin. "Oh! I assure you, he who gets this will have a bargain."

Both men became immediately desirous of possessing this talismanic purchase, and, for a time, there was quite a little war of words; nor was it finally settled till the pedler proposed to toss up the coin and thus decide. Having followed his suggestion, it fell to the lot of the elder Hessian, who paid his money, and seemed as delighted as a child with a new toy.

Having completed his mission, the pseudo-pedler departed, still denying himself the pleasure of a parting glance with the lieutenant-colonel, whose heart was, for the first time, in a slight degree hopeful. He remembered Captain Green, a handsome, bold fellow, with the courage of a lion, and his captivity seemed robbed of half its terrors. For the first time since his imprisonment, he slept soundly that night, after thanking God with a full heart.

CHAPTER XI.

"OH MOST WOEFUL SIGHT!"

It still wanted nearly a week of Christmas. Lady Walsingham had, however, set all the confectioners and bakers to work. Cards of invitation had been issued, and most of the prominent people of Trenton were invited, and looking forward with great expectations to the promised entertainment. Seamstresses and dressmakers were all engaged; parties had been sent to different points to collect flowers for decorations, and Walsingham House began to wear a gay and festive air.

Elsie had been as good as her word. On the afternoon that Molly spent in the hospital, she had been driven over and received by her aunt with a great show of cordiality, which was not all assumed.

"And only think, my dear, some of those charming officers will be here almost every evening. I declare I'm half in love with that splendid Hessian General myself—I am indeed; and if I were only a little younger—ah! me," and she sighed and laughed at the same time.

"Or, if I only had a thin waist," she continued, as her niece resigned herself to what was as unwelcome as it was inevitable, "I do believe he would fancy me. I expect you will make quite a sensation, my dear, and rob me of all my conquests. Well, it's but right, I suppose. I'm the fruit and you're the blossom, and a very charming blossom, too."

That evening General Rahl made his appearance with one of his staff. Never had Elsie appeared more radiantly beautiful. Her dress was like a summer cloud, so floating and ethereal. She looked scarcely a being of earth, as she came in, in assumed spirits—her cheeks delicately flushed, her eyes far exceeding in splendour and depth of colour the finest diamond.

If the General had any heart to lose, it most assuredly left him quite on that evening. His passion assumed a most serious character, and her graciousness made his bewilderment all the greater. He certainly never had looked for such kindness from her hands. She addressed her conversation to him—she dazzled, she captivated, she conquered, at once and entirely.

Molly might have been there, but she pleaded indisposition and had retreated, for the pedler had sent a little package by Elsie, and in it was a letter that Molly read and re-read many times that night, and kissed more than once, it may be guessed.

Elsie had surprised Molly by her high spirits that night.

"Did I wake you, dear?" she cried. "Well, it's to hear the good news. I was not to tell you till after eleven. Where do you think your brave captain is?"

Molly started up all in a tremour.

"Silly child! didn't I tell you it was good news?" laughed Elsie. "Well, then, he is on his way to Washington's camp; and, by this time, is across the river."

"The dreadful river!" shuddered Molly. "How could he cross! It is not frozen over."

"Don't you fear, little girl, but what he will manage it. He is such a bold, dashing spirit that I almost fell in love with him myself," and she sighed and murmured :—

"Poor Washburn! Dear—dear Harry!"

"The General asked me to visit the camp with my aunt and yourself, to-morrow. Molly, we must manage to see him," she said after a long pause.

"I dare say we shall," said Molly. "And I have thought of a plan."

"What is it?"

"I can't tell you to-night, because I have not quite finished it."

"Very well; to-morrow will do."

"One little knows what to-morrow will bring forth," replied Molly, sleepily.

"True! one little knows."

That to-morrow brought the General in style. A dashing barouche drew up to the door. Elsie shuddered as he gallantly took her hand to help her in. He was very chatty and pleasant during the short drive, entertaining them with stories of his campaigns.

They alighted at the camp. Elsie was now pale and anxious. She almost doubted her powers of self-control. How should she act in the presence of the man she loved and wished to save? What might he not suspect, seeing her in company of the Hessian General? If, by any means, he could be got to remain behind! She hardly saw what was passing before, around her, so absorbed was she in painful thoughts. She hardly heard the language and exclamations of her escort, and, at last, he noticed her languor. His fear that she was fatigued brought animation back, but it was only galvanic.

At last Molly broached the visit to the prisoner.

"It is his hour for exercise," said the General. "It may be as well to appear on the ground as chance visitors."

Elsie found it harder than ever to control herself. She had not thought much of how they would meet, only how she desired they might. It seemed to her that it would be in a room, or a tent, but this thrusting herself upon his notice as a total stranger under the escort of the man who, he must be cognizant that she knew, had condemned him to death, seemed needless cruelty. No chance for a communication, then. She felt a bitterness toward her aunt, who had refused the arm of the General in her favour, and under a pretext of keeping her long dress from soiling, she dropped his arm with an apology as they passed along.

"Yes: yonder he is with two guards," said General Rahl, and Elsie felt her very heart grow cold as they neared the place, and saw the tall, handsome figure of the lieutenant-colonel, between two stalwart Hessians.

Nearer they came and nearer. The prisoner kept his eyes on the ground, apparently determined they should see he did not wish to be made a spectacle of.

"I thought I remembered the name," cried Lady Walsingham. "Why, General—" a warning pressure and pleading look from Molly stopped her. The General had half turned—at that moment the prisoner looked up; his eyes encountered the pleading, almost passionate glance of the woman he loved. It was impossible for him to control himself. He started with a gesture of surprise, and an exclamation escaped him. The two guards instantly assumed a threatening aspect. Elsie grew faint with apprehension, and caught at the General's arm for support.

"Miss Vernon," he said, "I had no idea the sight of a prisoner would affect you like this."

"It is the thought—that—he is to die," she half gasped.

"Ah! I dare say; but we cannot reverse the decision with anything like honour. By the laws of war, spies are always executed. The commanders on the other side would have no mercy on me, if I were caught in the same offence."

"But are you sure he was a spy?" asked Elsie, in a low voice, that faltered somewhat.

"He has been judged and not acquitted," said the General, impressively. "His judges were fourteen of the best men in my command. But you are very much overcome by this visit, Miss Vernon. I regret that you came."

"I regret it myself. My temperament is a sensitive one, and I solemnly assure you I would do much to commute that man's sentence."

"Impossible," was the grave reply, and they returned home silently.

"We have failed," cried Elsie, "and something tells me that all is to end disastrously. Oh! Molly, what evil spirit tempted me to go?"

"Who would have dreamed that we should see him in that manner in the presence of all those soldiers?" Molly exclaimed, half pouting. "Even as it was, I attempted the alphabet, but he had no eyes save for you."

"Did he look at me again?" Elsie asked, mournfully.

"I had no heart to notice.'

"Indeed, he did! such a glance that brought the tears into my eyes. He really did not seem glad, as I thought he would."

"Can you wonder?" exclaimed Elsie, passionately, clasping her hands.

"Indeed, I thought he would be pleased," said Molly, simply.

"Don't you comprehend?" cried Elsie. "Suppose you were under sentence of death, unjustly, and you should meet your best friend in familiar companionship with the man who had signed your death-warrant?"

"Well, to be sure, I didn't think of that," said Molly, thoughtfully. "The fact is, I was so anxious to do my part that I noticed little else. But there is time, dear Miss Elsie; can we not try again?"

"Oh, Molly! there's a dead weight on my heart," cried Elsie, bursting into tears. "I can't conquer the impression that I have brought ruin upon the man of all the world I love the best. Oh! it was brought home to me so terribly! Death by the hangman's hand—just as they would kill a murderer. It is awful! it will kill me."

"It will do neither him nor yourself good to take on in that way," said Molly. "I tell you there is plenty of time yet—trust me. I will devise a way to rescue him. It only needs a brave heart and a determined will."

"Oh, Molly! don't try to comfort me; not a word you say gives me comfort."

Molly held her fingers up and telegraphed the one little word she had designed to force upon the attention of the prisoner.

"Do you forget," she said, gently, "that Captain Paul has gone over to the American army?"

Elsie shook her head. She forgot nothing, she said;

but that terrible impression remained—a cloud covered her very soul, and she could not see through it.

"It is silver-lined, nevertheless," said Molly.

CHAPTER XII

THE BETRAYAL.

Some ten or fifteen officers sat at supper. The table was furnished with a splendid silver service; glass and silver sparkled everywhere. Lawyer Asbury always gave sumptuous entertainments when he undertook anything of the sort. He was a good German scholar—his wife was of German descent; so there was no difficulty on the score of conversation, save to poor little Miss Lydia Lavoy, who, padded, painted, and furbelowed, stretched her long, lean neck hither and hither, and opened her faded, glassy eyes to their widest extent, as if that would help her in the mysteries of High Dutch.

"Does he mean me to take wine with him?" she cried, excitedly, to her hostess, who was babbling in an unintelligible language to her.

Mrs. Asbury nodded, and the poor *passé* belle acknowledged the compliment by sundry shrugs and nods, as she simperingly drank with a handsome young lieutenant.

"I say, Asbury," a middle-aged man who sat near the centre of the table called out, "have you heard the latest news?"

"About what?" asked the lawyer, who was disturbed in a *tete-a-tete* with General Rahl, and felt rather cross about it.

"Why, there has been a strange-looking German pedler about here for a day or two. Did any of you see him?"

"I did," volunteered Miss Lydia Lavoy. "I never heard of such prices!"

"Who do you suppose they say he is?" queried the middle-aged man again, ignoring Miss Lavoy, whose tongue was aching from its long confinement.

"How the deuce should I know?" answered the lawyer.

"Well, it's pretty well understood that it was Captain Paul Green, the widow Green's son," returned the middle-aged gentleman, who had grown quite red in the face.

By this time Mrs. Asbury had become interested.

"That accounts!" she exclaimed, exchanging looks with Miss Lavoy.

"Accounts for what?" asked the lawyer, in the tone he always assumed in addressing women.

"For the questions he asked. I saw him talking to the servants, the impertinent! and sent him off. But it is impossible it could be young Captain Paul Green, who is quite a handsome fellow, while this man was small, ugly, and almost humpbacked."

"I have it from the best authority," said the middle-aged gentleman, who, now he had turned the attention of the whole table toward himself, was slowly subsiding from crimson to his accustomed complexion.

"Pray, what did he question you about?" asked the lawyer of his wife.

"About affairs of which I knew very little, and, therefore, I could not answer him. Miss Lavoy had a long talk with him, however."

"I am sure, I hope you won't think, gentlemen, that I am in the habit of talking with every chance pedler who comes along," said Miss Lavoy, in considerable confusion, and addressing the staring Hessians, as if they understood every word she was saying. "I am not sure that I can quite recall what he did talk about, though chiefly, I think, it was the people at Walsingham House and Miss Elsie Vernon."

"What the deuce had he any business with the name of my niece?" queried the lawyer, in high dudgeon. "I wish I had heard him, I'd have kicked him out of the house."

Miss Lavoy was trembling now, for she really was afraid of Lawyer Asbury.

"They say he got into camp, too," continued the delighted middle-aged gentleman.

"In camp? Oh! no," responded the Hessian commander;" our rules are very strict. No wandering pedlers allowed within the limits."

"He most certainly did go there," continued the unsuspecting middle-aged gentleman, "for I have a German girl in my house who knows all about it, and he held communication with the condemned prisoner."

"It is a lie!" cried General Rahl, with an oath, for which he instantly, though hotly, apologized. "Nobody meddles with my guards; they know it is as much as their life is worth."

The middle-aged gentleman prudently held his tongue.

"I assure you that the man they speak of is a daredevil," said the lawyer, under his breath, to the General; "and what makes me think that this rumour may be true, is the significant fact of his speaking of my niece, Miss Elsie Vernon. It is not known by everybody, of course, but happens to be by my wife and myself, that Miss Vernon is engaged to Lieutenant-Colonel Washburn. I repeat, I should not wonder if there is something in it, or if my niece is at the bottom of the affair. Why, sir, she is such a confounded rebel, that she left my

D

house for the house of that vagabond's mother, the widow Green—she did, indeed, sir; and, possibly, she may have seen the Captain there—in the guise of a pedler, of course—and they together hatched some plan. She's a deep girl."

Not once had Lawyer Asbury glanced toward his guest as he sat making this ruinous speech—ruinous to all the hopes of the fair girl under discussion. Mrs. Asbury did, however, and wondered in her simple heart what the lawyer was saying to make his guest frown and turn pale like that—yes, actually pale, and gnaw his yellow moustache.

"It's frightful to see the man," she said to herself; "what can he be saying to him?"

"So, so!" said the General, when he had found his voice; "so, so!"

Something strange in the accent induced the lawyer to look up, and for the moment he was appalled. The Hessian's eye seemed rimmed with blood; a fierce and angry flush darkened his features, and all but distorted his countenance. Two or three of his officers, who knew that look, leaned back in consternation.

The General gulped down several glasses of wine, picked at the table-cloth in an absent way, but in a few moments had calmed himself.

"So the fair Miss Vernon is really engaged to my spy!" he said, with an attempt at a laugh, which set his officers busy with the dainties before them again.

"I have no doubt of it myself," said the lawyer, but his voice was not so even as it had been. He began to wish the middle-aged gentleman, who had volunteered the news, as far down in the Atlantic ocean as it was possible to be deposited. There was something so cruel in this suppressed passion of the man who was smiling beside him.

"She will lose her lover," said the General.

"Well—it will serve her right," responded the lawyer "I have often told her she was no niece of mine, supporting these rapscallions and enemies of their King. It will serve her right—of course, it will."

"Muehll, if we find our orders have been tampered with," said the General to one of his colonels, "the prisoner dies to-morrow."

The lawyer's cheek turned a shade paler. At that moment he felt very much like a murderer. The beautiful face of his niece seemed to stand before him, pale and bathed in tears.

Meantime the Hessian commander was secretly nursing his revenge. Now he saw through it all. His teeth came together as he remembered the interview, or what was scarcely that, between the prisoner and his fair charge.

"By heaven!" he said to himself, "I have been duped, but they shall pay dearly for it—very dearly. Yes, yes, I see it all, and the little girl is a hypocrite too! Perhaps they all are, Lady Walsingham into the bargain!"

Then again he went over the scene in the enclosure—the half-fainting condition of Elsie—and, as he now remembered, the perturbation of the prisoner.

"By heaven, he shall be hung to-morrow, at sundown," he muttered to himself, and Lawyer Asbury heard it. For the first time in his life he felt something like remorse.

The dinner went off rather soberly after that, for the General could not rally from the blow that had so unwittingly been given him. He grew moody and reticent. His nature had in it all the elements of revenge; and, surely, if anything could work them up, it was the feeling that he had been duped, in connexion with the violent passion he felt for the beautiful Elsie, whose charms had nearly turned his head, and quite conquered his heart.

After dinner there were cards, and a little music, and a little, nay, considerable, scandal. Miss Lydia Lavoy, remembering her belleship of many, many, years ago, tried to flirt with one and another—those who knew some little of English preferred.

"You like this country?" she asked of a red-faced, shock-headed German, whose hair took a tinge many shades more fiery than that of any individual present, and who had a habit of sending it standing all ways by thrusting his hand through it lengthways, crossways, and otherwise.

"Yaas—I likes it mooch as if dar' vas no snow," he replied, with a cheerful shove through the flame above mentioned.

"You don't like snow," said Miss Lydia.

"Nix," and he shook his head almost ferociously. "And I like not de beeples."

"The beeples—beeples?" muttered Miss Lavoy, inquiringly. "Might you mean—"

"De beeples, yaw—dat ish it, vat you haf' for kings—you call dem," he put in. "I no likes dem, not much—dey is not goot fighters, I no t'inks. Dey ish not got uniforms—not'ing at all, vat you would call like soldiers. Nix. I not like de beeples—de—beeples of this coontrie."

"Have you ever been to Lady Walsingham's?"

He shook his head.

"Don't you think our ladies are handsome ?"

"Ah !" he smiled most graciously, waving his hand in a graceful manner, " de-cideedlees !"

Mrs. Asbury was, meantime, arranging the table for cards, and making herself very agreeable, while her Tory husband followed the General, that he might find a chance to speak to him in private.

"Would it please you to smoke, General?" asked Asbury, as at last he cornered him. "I have some fine cigars imported expressly, and the smoking-room is quite private. If you prefer it, there are pipes and tobacco at your service."

The General thought he would smoke. Asbury rung and ordered some punch or other exhilarating beverage, and then escorted the General to a beautiful little apartment, fitted up quite in original style, the hangings and furniture of which had been imported. Here were pipes and cigars—smoking caps and slippers—pouches of tobacco —a tray, decanter and glasses, everything to please the fancy and minister to the taste.

The General sat down, but he seemed ill at ease. He tried a cigar and then a pipe, but seemed little satisfied with either. After frowning and making some little preliminary speech, he exclaimed :—

"So Miss Vernon is your niece."

"I regret to answer, yes," replied the lawyer.

"And a rebel."

"I regret to answer to that, also, yes."

"Pray, how does it come that she is with Lady Walsingham ? She does not seem to be affected by the notions of the common people."

"I really cannot tell you," said the lawyer, "what are her reasons, or what are Lady Walsingham's intentions.

Indeed, I have scarcely thought of her at all. She was very violent, and I dismissed her from my mind."

"She is an orphan?" queried the General, fiercely.

"Yes, General, and I regret to say that her father was a rebel before her, and instilled all kinds of free notions in his daughter's mind. I assure you I have tried my best to counteract these teachings, but she is incorrigible. Why, General, when some of the bare-legged troops of Washington and Lee were hereabouts, I have known her to walk ten miles to carry such things as woollens and refreshments. Ah! I can assure you it is in the grain; but, General—"

The latter looked up, moodily.

"I said she was engaged—the—matter may be broken off—I'm not certain."

"It is not likely to be broken off since she was there to see him," returned the General.

"What! the prisoner?"

"The prisoner," was the sharp reply.

"But—I don't understand."

"Through courtesy, of course. Your charming niece pretended to be a Royalist, and I admitted her to the—place of imprisonment."

"Just like her," muttered her uncle, "and that little plotter they call Molly was with her, most likely."

"Yes, she was with her."

"A cunning, pert little piece, the daughter of a farmer, who, to do him justice, is loyal. I wonder Lady Walsingham could consent to take her into service, for after all it comes to that. The little wench is pretty, you see, and smart, so that my sister is taken with her, and allows her to do anything. But, General—I think we understand each other."

"What the deuce do you mean?" queried General Rahl, with some asperity, not being in the best of humours.

"Elsie, though an obstinate girl, is possibly an ambitious one."

The General listened, moodily, as before.

"I think I could bring her round."

"Ah!" ejaculated the General, looking more animated.

"If you are particularly interested in her—why—"

"I am particularly interested in her," said the General, "I am very much interested in Miss Vernon, or was. I would have made Miss Vernon my wife. But she has acted with double dealing—with treachery worthy of a rebel. I am disappointed—very much disappointed," and the German puffed yet more furiously.

"Never give up," said the lawyer, whose spirits rose at this declaration, "women change their minds; they only want to be followed up."

The General shook his head.

"Miss Vernon has been guilty of duplicity, as I said before."

"Because she considered you her enemy."

"Because she loved that condemned rebel," and the General bit at his cigar furiously.

"Because it was very romantic," said the lawyer. "Depend upon it, a woman's heart must be taken by storm—she must be followed, pursued, if you please. This fellow must be made to act an important part."

"Ay! by releasing him?"

"No—by playing upon her fears. If you will do as I say—I will do as you wish. Her wish will be to have the sentence commuted—don't you see! She's a handsome girl, is Elsie."

"And you are a lawyer," laughed the General, who

had evidently taken heart. "Yes, yes, Miss Vernon is very beautiful. I believe I'll think over your advice. But I confess I was savage when you first intimated this matter about the officer under arrest. I felt as if I had been ill-used, and am not half sure yet but that I was. However, we will say no more about it. I am much obliged to you for your interest—particularly as you have given me renewed hope."

Seeing things under a more cheerful aspect, the General began to notice the really beautiful apartment, and soon entered into a discussion upon the comparative merits of German and English ideas of comfort. When they descended to the parlours, several of the officers had gone, but Miss Lydia had contrived to keep the fiery-headed lieutenant at her side—much against his will.

CHAPTER XIII.

THE NEWSMONGER'S CALL.

A GREY, gloomy day. Even Lady Walsingham caught the infection of dulness, and sat yawning, while Molly read to her. The room was what at Walsingham House was called the reading-room. It was lined very cosily with red, the furniture being of the same material and colour.

Elsie sat knitting some ornamental covering for the head. In the next room certain dressmakers were very busy with rich fabrics, and the cheerful hum of their voices could now and then be heard.

Elsie had never looked so charming, albeit the colour had faded from cheeks and lips. A certain suppressed pain in the lovely face only added to the interest to her appearance.

"What a **terrible** day!" cried Lady Walsingham, suddenly. "Throw down that book, Molly—it's very tiresome. Not that you don't read well, my dear, but it's insufferably dull. Oh, me! I wish somebody would come and bring some news."

"You're likely to have the first part of your wish, aunt," said Elsie, "for I think I see the Asbury carriage. Perhaps it's Aunt Emma."

"I don't care who it is; anybody will be welcome to-day," said Lady Walsingham, implying broadly her aversion to the lawyer's wife.

The carriage stopped at the gate—something in the likeness of a woman got out and hurried up to the door, the coachman holding an umbrella as she walked.

"Upon my word, it's Miss Lydia Lavoy!" cried Elsie, half laughing.

"Mercy!" was the startled exclamation of Lady Walsingham. "What can the creature want?"

"Oh, but, aunt, you said anybody would be welcome."

"She's nobody," returned the lady, pettishly. "Molly, you'll have to go and see to her, I suppose."

Molly stirred, not reluctantly, for she was not unwilling to see and hear something of this small piece of affected humanity; and in a few moments returned, with the prinking, smiling damsel of fifty, who with a youthful step and childish levity of manner, approached Lady Walsingham.

"You know I've been threatening," she said playfully, shaking the lace handkerchief she carried, "I threatened to come and stay with you a whole day. And, dear Lady Walsingham, if there's anything I can do, pray set me to work. I'm very handy, and my friends are pleased to commend my taste. My charming Miss Elsie, and how are you to-day?" she cried, tripping up to that young lady, and holding out a withered hand, that was still very small and white. "And oh! my dears, I've such news!"

So saying, she threw herself down on a great chair which Molly had placed for her, and totally ignored, by her position, all idea of the work she had asked for.

"Well, you must know, my dear friend, Lawyer Asbury, gave a dinner-party yesterday."

"Oh! we knew of that," said Lady Walsingham.

"Very true; I don't doubt it. It was a dinner exclusively for gentlemen, you see, and a very grand affair. I must say that Mr. Asbury understands how to give an entertainment of that kind the best of anybody it was ever my good fortune to know. Bless me! what a splendid thing!"

This exclamation was called forth by the entrance of a dress of crimson velvet, with a dressmaker behind it, and quite hidden by its broad folds. Lady Walsingham despatched it as soon as possible, and then composed herself to listen. Elsie was sitting now, with hands crossed on her lap, her eyes fixed on vacancy, or, at any rate, not appearing to see any object before her.

"Well, you must know the General and his staff were present—bless me! nothing more than a knot of stupid fellows, that is, to me, who could talk no German, and only sit and look on. Besides, what was there to hinder me from making awkward mistakes?

"Well, presently, do you think, somebody broached the idea that Captain Paul Green—that widow's son, you know—had been seen about. Mercy, child!" she added addressing Molly, "how you jumped!"

"Did I?" asked Molly demurely. "No wonder; I pricked my finger."

By this time Elsie had laid down her sewing, and was gazing no longer on vacancy, but at the little atomy, with a strange expression in her dark eyes.

"Yes; they declared that he was about as a spy, in a pedler's dress, and if it was him, I saw him, and, what is more, bought some of his trinkets. I thought he made himself uncommonly free with the names of people hereabouts—particularly yours, Miss Elsie."

"Mine!" echoed Elsie, faintly.

"Yes; and then the same guest declared that the pedler, or captain, or whatever he was, had been in camp, meddling with the prisoner, and you should have seen that Hessian's face as he thundered No! But the man insisted, and then Lawyer Asbury told some story or other to the General. I don't know what—and by the way, they say he is only General by brevet; that his real rank is that of colonel—however, a blacker or more fiendish face than he presented at that moment I never saw. He turned pale and then purple—upon my honour he did, and gnawed his under lip, until I really thought he was going to have a fit. It was terrible to see, and all the officers seemed to feel frightened — at least they looked so. By-and-bye he cried, with clenched hand—oh! and I forgot to tell you he swore, and gave the lie direct to his informer, which wasn't very gentlemanly—and then, says he, turning to one of his staff:—

"'If we find our orders have been tampered with, the prisoner dies to-morrow!'"

A deathlike stillness succeeded this communication. Elsie sat erect, like a piece of white marble. Molly had turned her head away; her arms hung lifeless.

"To-morrow—to-morrow! why, that means to-day!"

It was the voice of Elsie; but it sounded so unnatural

and far off, that even Miss Lavoy started at its ghost-like echoes.

"Oh, Miss Elsie!" cried Molly, a piercing anguish in her voice, "Could they have hung him this morning?"

"God knows!" was the reply, in that still sepulchral voice.

Molly gave a wild sob; Lady Walsingham frowned.

"See how you have set these children off with your improbable stories!" she exclaimed in real anger. "I don't believe a word of it, Elsie—that is—pardon me, Miss Lavoy, I think you misunderstood."

"I will pardon you, because I believe I have hurt and frightened you all; but I am not used to have my word doubted. I tell you I heard exactly what he said; and then, after that, I distinctly understood him to exclaim, 'He shall be hung to-morrow, at sundown!' I am sure who he meant, and I know by his face he will do as he said."

"Elsie has fainted!" screamed Molly, rising up, wringing her hands.

"No, I have not fainted," said Elsie, speaking with difficulty. "Excuse me—I—find I must leave you."

She arose, and leaning on Molly's arm, dragged herself from the room.

"I'm very sorry you should have told that dreadful story," said Lady Walsingham. "I believe my niece had a particular interest in Lieutenant-Colonel Washburn. It is an awful death to think of."

"But, indeed, I only told it as a piece of news," returned Miss Lydia, bridling. "I think, if I am to be considered a bird of ill-omen, I had better go back, and I would if I had not ordered Tapley to come at five."

"Oh, there is no necessity for that," returned Lady

Walsingham; "you are very welcome; only I didn't like to think of that poor man."

"Pray don't think of him, then. But, my dear friend, I believe I made a conquest last night. I really believe I did."

"Ah! you have made a great many conquests in your life, I suppose."

"Indeed I have, Lady Walsingham," returned Miss Lydia, bridling, "although I never took advantage of them. I may say my conquests have been too numerous to remember. I never shall forget the dear, fat old count, when we were at Marseilles. You should have seen him go down on his knees to me, and me having to help him up—the ridiculousness of the affair! But, then, perhaps, you never knew that I did come very near getting married once."

"No, indeed; I never heard of that."

"Of course not, for it was years ago; but I did. Ah, he was the handsome man for one to see—the handsome man. Nothing can I liken his eyes to but diamonds—so bright, and clear, and beautiful! I was but a child then—a mere child, and was, of course, captivated by his good looks. But he pretended to have immense estates, and was so rich! and he presented me with diamonds and precious stones, and my *trousseau* was all ready, real point-lace, and everything to match; real orange flowers, too—nothing sham; and the cake was made, the wine ordered, the cards out, the bridesmaids all come from long journeys—fourteen of them—the presents ready to display—and oh dear! it really makes me faint to think of it."

"Did he play bo-peep, and get locked up in a meal-chest?" laughed Lady Walsingham, indolently.

"No; I wish he had, for there would have been an end of it, and an honourable death in the bargain. No, no," and she shook her head pathetically; "my father found him out."

"Found him out?"

"Yes; and what do you think he was?"

"Some nobleman's valet, passing himself off for the real thing?"

"Oh, dear! no. He was a pedler—a miserable pedler, and all the diamonds were paste; and you can't think how that fellow who came to our house the other day reminded me of him. I couldn't resist the temptation of talking to him, it recalled so vividly the memories of past days."

"From that time I dare say you have voted all men deceivers," said Lord Walsingham, repressing a yawn.

"Yes, yes, there are so many looking after a little fortune, you see, that it has made me shy. But, Lady Walsingham, don't laugh if I tell you that I really did like that—that fellow; and if they hadn't driven him out of town, I might have been just romantic enough to run away with him. Oh! he did have such eyes!"

"Handsome as your new conquest last night?" Lady Walsingham did not conceal her yawn now. The day was dark, Elsie had gone away and in sorrow, and the monotonous, affected voice of Miss Lydia gave her the blues.

"Handsome! laws me; did you ever see a handsome German?"

"Oh, yes, plenty of them," was the reply. "General Rahl." Miss Lydia shook her head.

"Not to my liking. Dear, dear, who is that laughing so?"

"The servants, I think," said Lady Walsingham.

At that moment one of the girls come in with a note, which Lady Walsingham read and put aside.

"What are they laughing at, down in the hall?" she asked.

"A fortune-teller," replied the girl, on a broad grin.

"A fortune-teller!"

"Yes, sure. It's an old man came to the gate, askin' for bread or some'at to eat. So he said, would we like to have our fortunes told? And cook said she'd give him some dinner for it. So he's been at it, mum."

"An idea!" cried Lady Walsingham; "just the thing for this horrible day! Tell him to come up. You have no objections, Miss Lydia?"

"La! no!—I'm sure," was the nervous reply. And the girl was despatched below with orders to bring up the fortune-teller.

Lady Walsingham bestirred herself. It was so good to have a new sensation, with the dull rain coming down, and the dull face of Miss Lydia staring at her opposite, and the dull feeling generally that things were going wrong and she couldn't help it, that her spirits brightened somewhat. She gave a little fling with the duster, that sent an extra flare of yellow flame up the chimney; she re-arranged a marble shepherd on the mantel-piece, and almost hummed aloud, when the door opened, and there entered a man of a somewhat suspicious appearance, looking about him as if astonished to find himself in the midst of such splendours and luxuries. An old man, with keen, bright eyes, long, grizzled locks, and dressed in a faded blue blouse and faded brown trousers.

"So you tell fortunes, my good man?" said Lady Walsingham.

"Not much need to tell your fortune, my lady."

"And why?"

"You carry it in your face, my lady," with an admiring look.

Oh! nonsense!" But she flushed, and seemed pleased. "Well, how is it done? Do I cross your hand with silver? or do you tell by my hand and then I pay you?"

"I will see your hand." She held it out.

"Ah! fortune here and beyond the sea; a marriage with one you love. No trouble—every happiness. He will be tall, with black eyes and hair."

"And my fortune!" cried Miss Lydia, with a smirk.

"Ah! he is coming," laughed the man. "He is not tall; he has light hair and he loves you very much. Riches, of course."

"Mary," said Lady Walsingham to the girl, who still lingered at the door, "tell Miss Elsie and little Molly I want them."

Only Molly came, distress in her face—came to excuse Elsie and herself. On the instant, seeing the old man, a strange light brightened her face—an expression she tried to control and darken. Her lips trembled; she seemed undecided.

"And your fortune," said the voice; "hold your hand out."

She obeyed, passively.

"It is all coming right!" said the old man, looking her steadily in the eye—"everything. Do you understand? There is trouble here—but it will be lightened soon. You are feeling bad, thinking somebody is going to die; he will not die, if it is a man—she will not die, if it is a woman."

Molly felt herself growing strong, taking hope. She knew who was under this disguise—knew what the vague words meant, and, running laughing up-stairs, while Lady Walsingham paid the man, she cried, hysterically, bursting into Elsie's presence: "I have seen Paul, and Paul will save him!" But Elsie would not be comforted. "But I have seen Paul; I knew him in a moment. Be sure he has heard all about it."

"No, never, that he is to be hung so soon. Don't speak to me, Molly; I shall go distracted, I know I shall."

"But I know Paul will do something," said Molly, half beside herself at the frantic way Elsie went on.

"Don't say Paul to me again," retorted Elsie. "You must be out of your head. If it had not been for him, this never would have happened. Remember it was his going there and being found out about it that incensed General Rahl. Don't speak of it again—don't mention Paul's name."

Molly felt hurt, but forbore to comfort her for a long time, knowing that it was grief made her seem unkind.

CHAPTER XIV

THE SACRIFICE.

"OH! Miss Elsie, indeed, you must not give way so; it may not be true," cried Molly, when Elsie began mourning again.

"It is true, Molly. Oh! my God! it is true! My uncle must have told him all. He would have felt a particular delight in doing me an injury of that kind. Oh! how cruel! how cruel! Molly, I have taken my last look at him. His noble face, so pale, so accusing, will haunt me for ever. Oh! that cruel, cruel Hessian!"

Elsie had thrown herself, in very agony, on the floor, by the bedside, and lay crouched there, white and tearless.

She had not heard Miss Lavoy's correction, that the soldier was to be hung at sunset, for at that instant she had nearly fainted.

"Molly, I doubt not he lies dead even now, stretched on some cold floor. Oh! the thought distracts me! Why could I not have known? Could not some good and pitying angel have told me in my dreams? I would have tried to see this wicked General. I would have begged the boon of his life on my knees. Molly, I would have sold myself for him. Oh! I would! I would!"

"Miss Elsie, you don't know what you are saying," groaned Molly.

"I worshipped him so—I worshipped him so! God forgive me, he was my idol; and even then he did not seem half so dear to me till now. Oh! my love! my love!—my dead, dead love!"

"Miss Elsie, oh! what can I say to comfort you?" wailed Molly, at her wits' end with sympathy and grief.

"Nothing, nothing; don't try. Let me mourn by myself—let me die. Indeed, I cannot support this burden and live."

"How do you know he is not living?" asked Molly.

"How do I know? You heard her say yourself that he was to be hung to-morrow. How gratify his base purposes better than by putting him out of the way as soon as possible!"

"If she did, so I heard her say that he spoke again, and declared he should be hung at sunset. You were faint, perhaps, and didn't hear."

"I was faint one moment. Everything seemed passing from me—her voice and all. Oh! Molly, are you sure she said that?"

"Sure," repeated Molly.

"Then there is some hope."

"Yes, while there is life," replied Molly.

"What shall we do?" and Elsie lifted herself from the floor. "Something must be done. What shall we do?"

"I wish I knew what to advise," said Molly; "but do you know, I think he dare not do such a thing."

"Oh! darling, these Hessians know no mercy. How can you think it? I cannot help seeing from this man's actions what he thinks of me; and, God forgive me, I have led him on, I fear, hoping that I might help *him*. Now, jealousy is added to his other base passions. Till sunset," she added, "till sunset. Oh! the precious hours! they must not be lost! We must manage to get to the camp, Molly—we must see the General; suspense will kill me. He must not die!" she cried, with passionate fervour. "Oh! my God! this once grant me his life!"

A servant knocked.

"My lady's compliments," she said, with a low curtsey; "General Rahl is below stairs."

"Is not your prayer almost answered?" cried Molly, the tears in her bright eyes, as the girl went out.

"Oh! it looks like it. Yes, he has come, and we did not hear," continued Elsie, going to the window. "There is his horse. I must see him alone. Oh! how shall I plead?—what shall I say?"

"Don't fear, my dear Miss Elsie," whispered Molly. "The words will come; let me help you. What are you doing?"

"Looking for another dress," was the reply, with a haggard smile. "I wish to appear my best before this awful Hessian. Am I very pale? How shall I hide the traces of tears?"

"They'll all be gone before you go down. There, now,

I'm sure I should never know. It's a dark day, you see, and there's no great light comes in those windows, with the curtains down. God help you, my dear Miss Elsie; I'll pray for you every minute."

Elsie went down slowly, very slowly, wondering whether her aunt was there, and if she could command herself sufficiently to control her emotions if there should be no hope.

General Rahl met her, *suave* and bland, as usual. If he noticed the trembling of her hand, he did not appear to, and she suppressed the loathing his presence occasioned.

The conversation, in the beginning, was on ordinary topics. Not the first time that the mere praise or blame of a day has covered a heart-break.

"Miss Elsie, I have come on a strange errand," at last spoke the Hessian.

Elsie's pulses were flying now.

"We may not have a great while to stay here," he went on, "as Sir William Howe is expected soon, with fresh troops, and that will necessitate a movement on our part. We shall hem the American army in and crush this rebellion before another spring."

Everything now was subordinate in the mind of Elsie to the effort she wished to make for the life of young Washburn, or she would have sprung indignantly from her seat and hurled her defiance upon the enemy of her country; but this was not the time, when a life so dear trembled in the balance.

"Miss Elsie, I do not know how to make love," he said, immediately after, with a gesture of embarrassment. "I am a plain man in my way, but I have never seen the woman yet to whom I could so truly say, 'I love you, as to you.'"

Elsie was silent; her eyes were downcast; her soul was in array against every word he uttered.

"General Rahl," she said, "I will be frank with you; my heart is no longer in my own keeping."

"Ah! it was true, then," he muttered, his heavy brows coming together. "And I, Miss Elsie, will be equally frank with you; you are affianced to a condemned criminal."

Her eyes shot fire.

"To a hero, who will die a martyr and a patriot!" she cried, all the love of country uppermost at that moment.

"I have to wish you a good morning," he said, and there was either actual sorrow or a sneer in his deep voice.

"Oh, General Rahl!"—she stood before him, barring his progress, beautiful and in tears. He paused.

"You will not be so cruel," she cried; "he never injured you. Oh! if you love me, as you say, you will never be so cruel."

"I can and will be—not cruel—but just. The man has friends who may have been in communication with him. He must die."

These words he said almost savagely, and as if between his closed teeth.

"What can I do to save him!" she cried, wringing her hands. "What can I do, General Rahl?"—and she made a motion as if to fall upon her knees, but he saved her the humiliation, by leading her almost forcibly to a seat.

"I pity your anguish, Miss Vernon, but your lover is doomed."

"Who told you he was my lover?" she cried.

"Do you deny it?" and he looked her steadily in the face.

"General Rahl—you are very cruel."

"So you have said once before; but it rests with you entirely. I make this concession in pity to your feelings. Whether this renegade is your lover or not—it rests with you whether he is hung in eight hours, at the setting of the sun."

"With me?" cried Elsie, staring at him vaguely.

"Entirely with you. I have told you that I love you If you wish to save him, become my wife."

"Now—so soon? I am bewildered; you can't say now."

"Not this moment, certainly, as I am a consistent Churchman, and no preparations have been made. But soon, certainly."

"And that will save him?"

"I pledge my honour as a soldier, that will save him."

"You will not hang him at all?"

"He shall not be hung."

"But soon, you say—how soon?"

"I should like it to be on Christmas night, at this party of your aunt's."

"No, no," and she almost gasped, "not on Christmas night. My father died on a Christmas night—my only sister died on Christmas night—no, no—not then;" she shuddered as she spoke.

"The next day?" he pleaded.

She caught at the respite.

"It is so soon—and I am so unprepared!"

"You need make no extra preparations—yourself is all I want. Am I answered?"

"And Lieutenant-Colonel Washburn goes free?" she queried, tremblingly.

"I did not say that—I said he should not be hung."

"Or shot?"

"Miss Vernon, you press me close," he said, after a pause; "do you doubt my word of honour as a soldier?"

He had turned pale.

"You have said so often that, by the rules of war, a spy must die—not that I consider that he is a spy," she added a little haughtily.

"And have I not also said that the pardoning power lies with the Commander-in-Chief?"

"But you have not told me he shall not be shot," said Elsie, calmly.

For a moment a glance of rage kindled his eye. He seemed to reflect.

"Since you doubt my sincerity, Miss Vernon," he said, again, "I tell you he shall be neither hung nor shot. Is that sufficient?"

"It is," said Elsie, who felt herself growing cold as he drew near her.

"And I may depend upon your promise?"

She drew herself up proudly.

"I shall neither run away nor take poison, General," she said, with a firm voice. "If you are willing to wed me after the assurance I have given you, I shall fulfill my promise if you come for me on the day after Christmas."

"I certainly shall come," was his response. "Farewell."

He had the good sense not to kiss her as they parted.

Molly met Elsie at the head of the stairs.

"Has it ended well?" she asked.

"We shall see," was the cold response.

"Oh! Elsie, what has happened? What makes you so calm and so cold?"

"I am so cold," said Elsie, shivering. "Lead me in—I believe I have almost lost my strength."

Molly led her to the fire.

"It is very foolish, but I believe my teeth are chattering," said Elsie, with an attempt at a laugh.

"Oh! Elsie, you frighten me," cried Molly, with a shudder.

"Don't be foolish, Molly; you ought to rejoice—I have saved him!"

"Saved him! But, good Father! how white you look—there—I won't say a word, if it distresses you."

"I'm to be married the day after Christmas, Molly—wish me joy!"

"Oh! Elsie—I'm crying, instead. Not till the day after Christmas?" she suddenly exclaimed. "Glory, hallelujah."

"Why, what is the matter with you?" and Elsie turned with some interest in her hitherto passive face.

"Matter with me—why! you're both saved, to be sure. Isn't it on Christmas night I'm to carry out my little plan? To be sure it is. After Christmas—thank God on your knees that it's not before."

Elsie shook her head.

"I don't see anything in it, Molly; I don't see anything but sacrifice, and then, perhaps, death."

"Pooh!" cried Molly, with energy—"sacrifice and death. Nonsense! I tell you there's no danger that my plan will go wrong; only try to be cheerful—try to believe in me. I've not quite perfected my little plot, but it's a good one. Now, depend upon it—you'll be Mrs. Washburn before you're Mrs. Rahl. Mrs. Rahlpah! what a name! It never shall fit you, that I'm determined on."

Elsie could but take courage from the energy with which little Molly discussed her plans. After all, matters were not as bad as they might be. Sunset would not see the body of him she loved dangling like a common felon from a tree; and, by Christmas, something might ensue to prevent the dreaded consummation.

"It's the best thing that ever happened, that poor old spinster coming here to day," continued Molly. "Suppose you had not heard the news?"

"Heaven knows what might have been the consequences!"

"And so do I," cried Molly, pertly; "Mr. Hessian would have been snubbed, and have gone home with a death-warrant in his eyes, while you'd been none the wiser. I'm going down to cosset that old maid, out of gratitude."

CHAPTER XV.
CAPTAIN PAUL'S RUSE.

"AFTER incredible hardships, mother, here I am; make the most of me, for I shall only stay to-night."

The speaker's garb and the speaker's voice seemed strangely incongruous. The one was firm, cheerful, youthful—the other decrepit, careless, and more like a beggar than anything that had a home.

The man stood in the midst of the large room. Every curtain was down, every shutter shut, the doorway was locked; extra precautions had been taken, so that the widow's house, standing out there that bleak night, amidst the bare, skeleton-like trees, seemed quite deserted.

But it was not. On the contrary, the pleasant parlour

seemed full of a golden vitality. The flame in the chimney-place was steady and yellow, and sent light everywhere, from corner to corner. Tabby, the great tortoise-shell cat, blinked and purred, and sometimes moved her comfortable quarters to others not less comfortable, taking a circuit round the new-comer's legs, and rubbing lovingly against them.

In the middle of the room stood a table, covered with a snow white cloth, and set with ancient china, which the widow's sailor-husband had brought home years ago; honey in the centre; wheaten loaf next; yellow butter; crisp, whitish crullers; well-cooked and cut ham, and now the widow's woman came out of the kitchen, bearing tea-urn and hot biscuit.

"You used to scold me for being such a mimic," continued the figure, lifting a bunch of grizzled hair from his head, to which was attached, somehow, a string of false beard, "but you see it has served me in good stead. Remember how I used to take you off, Hannah?" he queried, turning to the woman, who was smiling at his odd appearance.

"Don't I?" was her response; "and how I tried to pay you for it, many's the time."

He laughed heartily at the recollection of his boyish scrapes, and soon stood before them—Paul Green—a handsome, stalwart, and yet lithe young man.

"Ah! the scrapes are not quite ended yet," said the widow, sighing, and smiling; "no knowing what they will bring thee to yet."

"To honour, mother mine. You should have seen Washington when he thanked me. Why, there was promotion in the very curve of his lips. I'll be lieutenant-colonel yet, please God."

"And how does Washington stand it?" asked the widow.

"As nobody but himself could," was the reply. "Trouble doesn't seem to wear him down in flesh. His eye is as calm, and his countenance as genial as ever. He's a trump, is our General!"

"And how does he think the war is going?"

"Oh! he is always hopeful, though he doesn't say much. There's no doubt but we'll pull through, and drive these scurvy fellows from our shores. But oh! the poor soldiers! I wish I was rich, mother."

"Ah! a many of us wish that, but wishing does no good. It seems sad to think that most of the wealth is on the side of our enemy. There's Lawyer Asbury, rolling in riches, they say, and Lady Walsingham going to give such a Christmas as never was given here yet, costing thousands, perhaps, while our poor soldiers perish with cold. Indeed, I do wish I were rich; but, alas! as I said before, wishing does no good. But sit down, child, and take some supper.

The child—somewhere near six foot, and of proportionate breadth, sat down, but seemed even more inclined to talk than to eat.

"What's become of thy appetite?" anxiously asked his mother.

"Why, to tell the truth, I do believe I'm not hungry," he said, leisurely buttering his bread, "for I took a late dinner up at Walsingham House."

Both Mrs. Green and Mrs. Green's woman stared at him, after this speech; the latter, always privileged in the parlour, knitting away at the side of the fire.

"What do you mean, my son?" asked widow Green.

"I mean what I say; I was at Walsingham House,

and the cook gave me some dinner for telling the maids' fortunes."

"Now, if I ever!" cried the pleased sewing-woman, rapturously holding forward the stocking she was busy upon.

"But what for there!"

"Oh! I had a purpose," said Captain Paul, blushing a little.

"To see the girl, of course," said widow Green's woman, nodding.

"Yes, partly that. Mother, what a pretty little thing Molly is; don't you think so?"

"Well, middling," said the widow, gravely.

"Oh! now, mother, be honest; say that she is almost as handsome, though without her grand way, as Miss Elsie herself."

"A pretty thing—a pretty thing," said widow Green's woman, nodding again. "But, I should think you would be afraid of being caught."

"Not much; though there's a rope ready for me, saying I should be. Now, mother, none of that," for the old lady had put her apron to her eyes. "Wait till it happens before you cry for me, and when it does, I'll give you full leave. But that'll never be. I can outrun the 'swift gazelle' himself, and cheat the—well, I won't say who, before present company. But, I tell you, I rather like Lady Walsingham, enemy or no enemy. She has such a wholesome, natural way of doing things; and then, she's so kind to Molly. You'd better believe that I had a good time to-day, and made two or three dollars in the bargain—Hark!"

"What is it?" cried widow Green, while her woman started to her feet, looking fiercely about.

"Nothing; only I fancied I heard steps—not likely, though. And such fortunes as I gave them! I wonder if any of them will ever come true?"

"But what else did you do?"

"Told Lady Walsingham's fortune."

"Oh! Paul, you didn't do that!"

"Didn't I though? And a right handsome woman is Lady Walsingham. Beside her was a small piece of antiquity, upon whom I almost expected to find the label—

"'This is a Mummy.'

"For her I prophesied a husband—'pon word! and she looked as pleased as could be. Then breathing a parting warning into Molly's ear, bless her bright eyes! what I specially went there for—I came away."

"Oh, Paul, it seems to me as if you put your life in danger for such trifling things!"

"Not trifling to me, mother. I thought I heard steps again—close against the windows," he said, speaking in a lower voice.

"Oh, my son, if they should suspect!—these dreadful Hessian soldiers—they would kill us all. Somebody told me the General heard that you had been tampering with the prisoner, and he is master mad with you."

"Who told you?"

"I can't say now—somebody at meeting the other Sunday. I know it frightened me not a little, and I trembled in my shoes to see you here to-night. Suppose we put out the candles?"

"Nonsense!" he said, lifting the glass full of honey, and spreading some over his bread.

"Mother, this tastes as it used to when I was—." He paused again, turning his face to the closed window. They were all silent and fearful. He arose from his chair, went to the window, put his ear against the inside shutter, and shook his head threateningly, as he said: "There's somebody there, I'm not mistaken; the ears of a good scout seldom are."

"Then we are lost!" cried widow Green.

"Nonsense!" cried her son.

"I've courage plenty for myself, but none for thee," she said, again.

The captain stood in a listening attitude against the shutter, while Mrs. Green's woman stole softly into the outer room.

"There are two or three of them," whispered the man.

"Of whom?"

"That I don't know. They are going softly round the west corner. The frost betrays them, though. Are you all fastened up?"

"Every part; we went from garret to cellar."

"Good; now get me my razor. My beard feels uncomfortable, what little there is of it."

"Your razor, Paul!" cried the widow, in a frightened voice.

"Yes, mother, and in a hurry. I've a plan in my mind."

She brought him the box containing his razors, trembling and wondering. He went through the process deftly and quickly; then, going to the fire he sought for a dead coal, and made a dot on his right cheek, changing his eyebrows with the same material. Then he parted his hair in the centre, and turned round to his astonished mother.

"Good gracious, Paul! you look like—"

"Get one of her caps as quickly as you can," interrupted the captain.

The widow started. The voice was as like that of her sewing-woman as if it had been herself. Dimly she comprehended that her boy was intending to bring his imitative powers into requisition, for the purpose of deceiving the enemy, if, indeed, they were outside. She brought the cap, while her woman was still reconnoitering, and he put it on, when his appearance was so exactly like the good stout sewing-woman, with a hair mole on the right cheek, and heavy brows, that the widow Green, in spite of the formidable nature of the circumstances surrounding them, burst into a laugh that, though she suppressed its hilarity, made her sides ache.

Presently in came her woman, with a bundle on her arm. She held up her hands, and raised her eyebrows, but did not laugh.

"It seems he has the same thought I have myself," she said. "Here are some of my clothes, and if my twin sister was alive, I'd say that's she. Now put them on; take my knitting, which you can do as readily as I can unless you've forgotten, and sit down by the fire. I'll manage the rest."

"Then there is somebody outside?" said the widow.

"Ay; more than one somebody—three somebodies—five somebodies, and one or two of 'em soldiers, with their yellow thingumbobs on their shoulders. I was bound to see, and the mercy knows how long it took me to lift my window as softly as softly could be, and then manage a crack in the shutter, so that they needn't see. They were talking in a whisper when I saw them, and, Lord forgive me, if I didn't wish for a kittle o' boiling water, for I had a smart chance to pour it right over 'em. It's no doubt they'll break out soon, for they've likely tracked him here, and more likely have heard him talking and laughing. Now, if he ain't greatly changed from what he used to be, he can mimic me, looks and voice, enough to take my clothes and jest slip 'em on. If they get boisterous, and will come in, why I'll let 'em on, or he will, and when they're safe in the house, I'll slip out and go over to my son's. It's growing bitter cold, and I guess they'll be glad of a warm fire, after sneaking around there in the wind."

"What, they come in and be right here? No, no," said the widow, tremblingly.

"Don't you be in the least afraid for me," returned Captain Paul; "only you keep your wits about you, mother, and I'll be sure to have mine. I like the fun hugely," he added taking up the bundle, and preparing to go. "If I don't fool the codgers, then there's no fool in me. Aha?"

There came a knock at the door at that moment—a very quiet knock.

"Their knuckles will get desperately cold," said Captain Paul, and hurried out to array himself, while Hannah concealed the clothes and disguise he had worn there about her person. "Say nothing in answer to the raps yet," he whispered, through the door; "make them something hot."

This, also, Hannah had thought of, and was now preparing over the fire. She also brought on the table extra glasses, and a jug steaming hot.

Again the knock was repeated—this time with more decision. A second Hannah now stalked in, seated herself by the side of the fire-place, and caught up that damsel's work, which lay on a chair.

"Not that I'm going to let you spoil that," cried the real Hannah; and, going to the drawer, she brought out the ravelled half of a stocking, changed the needles dexterously, and he went to work amid much suppressed laughter, for the sight was a ludicrous one whenever the two Hannahs spoke to each other.

"Let 'em rattle about for awhile," said the real widow Green's woman; "they'll git impatient pretty soon, I guess, and then we'll have to—"

A tremendous thumping at the front door put an end to the sentence.

"I'll go up," said Hannah.

So she went to the room above, made a great noise at the shutters—delayed over raising the window, and finally put her cap-frill out, as if she feared that somebody might shoot her.

"Who's there?" she called. "Who disturbs two lone women at this time o'night?"

"You must come down and let us in, good woman," said a voice.

"Don't good woman me—be off; this ain't a tavern."

"We are very well aware of that," said Lawyer Asbury, who was the chief spokesman; "but, let me tell you that our business admits of no delay. There is an enemy of the King hidden in this house, and we have warrants to search it."

"Which of us two old women do you want?" asked Hannah, in a voice of scorn, determined to prolong the interview as skilfully as she could.

"Neither of you old women. Let us in, and we'll tell you who we do want. We've been pummeling here for an hour, now."

"It's pretty business, I think, a-going about frightening lone people such times as these. How do I know but you'll murder us all?"

E

"If you keep us here much longer you'll be sorry for it, old lady; so you had better hurry before we break the door in."

"Well, well, if you must, you must," replied Hannah; "but, make allowance for age, if you please; and rheumatiz—which I hope to the gracious the frost'll give you;" she muttered, laboriously pulling the window down, and closing the shutters.

Then she went down-stairs.

"Now, honey," she said, addressing the captain, 'make your best of me. I'll steal out while they're all here—out of the side-door, which, likely, they won't think of. They'll have somebody at the back one I suppose. Do you go to the front door with a candle and open it. And remember that I've had a hard time opening the winder up-stairs, and shettin' it, and that I've got the rheumatiz badly." Saying this Hannah walked off in the dark and watched her chance.

Captain Paul went to the door, and, after many groanings and some awkwardness, at last opened it, when in filed five men, the lawyer at their head.

"Laws now!" cried the pseudo-Hannah, "what has the millingtery come to do here, this hour o' night?"

"To find a traitor and a spy, you witch you; we've got him fast, too, I think, for let me tell you we shall search the house thoroughly."

"S'arch and welcome," was the reply; "there's nobody here but me and the mistress. Me you have always known, Lawyer Asbury—the mistress you has always known heretofore, as a good woman and church-going."

"Hold your palaver," muttered the lawyer, while Captain Paul made a grimace behind his back.

They went into the kitchen, where the widow, outwardly calm, but inwardly in much pertuberation, sat knitting.

"Widow, where is the fellow?" queried the lawyer. "We heard him talking, but now."

"What fellow?" queried the widow, while Hannah fell to mixing some hot spirits.

"No need of feigning, old lady," returned the lawyer, after saying something in German to one of the soldiers, "he was followed here direct to this door, and a guard put on so that we are perfectly sure he has not got out. You had better confess."

"Here's nobody but Hannah and I. You may search the house as soon as you please." The lawyer looked at her steadily. He was used to reading countenances, and on hers he read indifference.

"Well, we shall be obliged to search," he said, nodding to the soldiers.

"Have something hot?" asked Hannah, grating the nutmeg in a pitcher.

"Well, yes; the fellow can't escape us now. I don't care if I do." The soldiers were well pleased. Before the cheerful fire of the hospitable widow, even if they had come with evil intent, was pleasanter to the inner and outer man than standing in the frosty air with the mercury down to zero. So they drank the heating mixture and smacked their lips.

"Now, girl, give us plenty of light," said Asbury, "and show us every part of this floor. You, corporal, stay here with the widow, and look sharp."

"Now for up-stairs," said the lawyer, returning, and up they went, finding no contraband articles, although they poked their guns and long swords here, there, and everywhere. There was no cellar, so the kitchen and outhouses came in for their share, but of course nothing was found. The real Hannah had made good her escape.

"This is outrageous!" cried the lawyer. "I am sure the fellow came here, was tracked up to the very door, was heard talking, plainly, and in spite of our close watch, he has vanished. The house has been searched thoroughly. Widow Green, you are a church-member, and won't lie."

The widow looked up, alarmed.

"I'll lie for her," said Hannah, emphatically, "if it's lying you want. I'm no church-member, and it won't hurt me." The idea tickled the shrewd lawyer, and he smiled in spite of himself.

"We will put a guard round the house, at all events," said the lawyer.

"What! you keep us all in the house, and to-morrow market day?" cried Hannah.

"Oh! no; you or the widow are welcome to go out, but that fellow must be lurking somewhere here, and must be found. Widow Green, you say you've had no strange company to night."

"I didn't say so, but I do say so now," replied the widow.

"No man here to supper, eh?"

"Oh! yes, half a dozen," spoke up Hannah, ironically. "Didn't you hear 'em carousing and singin' and whistlin'? Of course two lone women expect to be insulted by such questions," and her needles quivered with anger.

"We all know that the widow has a son," said the lawyer.

"Well, ain' she a right to!" snapped Hannah.

"Nobody questioned that," responded the lawyer, who was afraid of Hannah's tongue, so well counterfeited.

"Then let her alone; its bad enough to have the boy off nobody knows where, fighting them—well I'd like to say devil's own foreigners, but I didn't. How can we tell if the poor fellow ain't laying bleeding somewhere 'twixt this and New York? Get along with you, Lawyer Asbury. You're in comfort; let other folks be, won't ye?"

"Well, I'm going," said the lawyer, taking one final gulp at the hot drink, "but I know that fellow came in here, and I know he hasn't gone out. At the same time, I know he's a traitor and a spy. Good-night. I'll leave a soldier here on your hospitality."

"What! one o' them he'then!" bounced Hannah—"why, we can't understand him."

"Can't help it; those were the orders;" and the men left, all but the corporal, who applied himself to drink.

When they were gone, the widow, at a sign, arose, and gave Hannah a candle; the two left the corporal sitting before the fire. It is needless to say that Hannah was allowed to go out the next day with her market-basket, that the basket contained a suit of men's clothes, and that the real Hannah returned.

CHAPTER XVI.

CAPTAIN MOLLY'S PLAN.

CHRISTMAS drew near. Everything was prepared for the grand festival at Walsingham House. The dresses were all made. Three or four rooms had been skilfully thrown into one by the substitution of curtains for doors, and these, looped back, gave a very pretty glimpse of the elegant stretch of apartments, all brilliantly illuminated, as they were to be on Christmas Eve, that the lady of the house might judge of the effect, which was very splendid.

The Delaware in some parts was quite frozen over, and there was good skating on the little stream that separated the upper from the lower village of Trenton.

Molly had grown very reticent of late. She seemed to have numerous errands across the river.

"I want to wear a gold necklace to-morrow night," she said, as she sat with Lady Walsingham.

"That you can easily do, child," replied the latter. "I have two or three, and Elsie will not wear hers."

Elsie sat in the next room learning to play chess. Her *vis-a-vis* was General Rahl, who was more and more infatuated with each succeeding interview. The General devoted all his spare time to Walsingham House, and, as he was one of the most prudent of men, and did not press upon her many lover-like attentions—moreover, as the Lieutenant-Colonel was not to be hung, Elsie saw more of his good qualities, and almost forgot to detest him.

"But I don't want yours, or Miss Vernon's," said Molly, "thanking you all the same. I want one of those old-fashioned necklaces of big beads, and nobody has one that I know of, but the widow Green."

"It seems to me you are infatuated with the widow Green," said Lady Walsingham. "I warn you that, if you have any feeling for that renegade son of hers, I shall see your father."

"Why, Lady Walsingham, you can't think that at my age, I could have a lover," said Molly, with an appearance of great ingenuousness. "Look back at your own girlhood. Remember, I am only seventeen!"

Lady Walsingham said nothing. At the age of seventeen she had already flirted with and discarded a half-dozen lovers.

"I know she'd lend them to me," soliloquised Molly;

"and don't I wish I could be transformed into a boy with a pair of skates on. Wouldn't I be over the river? I might send a note for them," she added.

"Yes, child, if you want them so badly, send by one of the servants," said Lady Walsingham; "though I don't believe any of them can be spared."

The next day Molly made her appearance in the kitchen, where she was a general favourite.

"Why, how busy you all are!" she cried.

"We has to be busy to-day, miss," said the butler. "Eight turkeys, two geese, sixteen chickens, three roast pigs, a side of mutton, and a quarter of beef. Joe, you rapscallion, attend to your work."

"An idle good-for-nothing," cried the cook, and Joe dodged a rolling-pin still keeping his eyes on Molly's face.

"Oh! Mr. John," said Molly, "how well you are looking!"

"Be I, miss?" queried the delighted butler.

"How I should like to see you on the ice; you would make such a grand figure." The latter was obese.

"I'm particular proud o' my calves, miss, particular proud o' my calves," he said.

"I wish you could skate, now—I've a little errand across the river."

"Couldn't, miss, couldn't," said the butler, his countenance falling. "Heft o' this Christmas dinner falls on me, though cook would dispute it," he added, more softly.

"Then, can't you spare somebody? Here's Joe—it wouldn't take him long, you know. It's only a note to carry."

"Them there Hessians would git hold of it. He's a fool—and it might be reason. Reason's mighty bad."

"Treason, John, you mean. But here; you may read it yourself—every bit of it."

Now, John could not read, and the witch knew it. He took it, however, with an important air.

"Oh! but, Mr. John, you've got it upside down."

"So I has, miss. I was jest going to turn it. You see, my sight is so shorted like. Ah! I see. Joe," he added, after due inspection, "take this note across the river for Miss Molly."

"I'll pay you for your trouble, Joe," said Molly.

"Does I want pay?" cried Joe, indignantly. "No, I don't. Ain't I grateful? Yes, I be! Wouldn't I go to Chiny for you? I would;" and on went his old wool-cap, with the missive snugly tucked inside.

Nearly two hours passed. Joe returned with the chain, but by sundry nods and shrugs, Molly saw that he had something of importance to communicate. Presently, she had ripped up the lining of his sleeve, and taken a note from thence.

The two girls were closeted together after Joe had been sent off with a large reward, and many words of caution. Then Molly warily opened the note. It was written by the widow Green, and ran thus:—

"Dear Little Molly,—I have heard from Paul. There will be stirring times between this and to-morrow, if all turns out well. In case of any trouble, you know where to come. Fortunately, the river is covered with solid ice. Be brave as ever, and trust in God. I dare not say more, except that thou must use thy woman's wit, to keep the Hessian officers as late as possible at the frolic. A word to the wise is sufficient."

"Elsie, that means something!" cried Molly, her cheeks crimsoned by excitement.

"Yes," said Elsie. "Oh, Molly—only to-morrow!"

"Elsie, are you sure you have the pass-word? How did you get it?"

"With a kiss," said Elsie, shuddering, "and I have hated myself ever since. It was a Judas' kiss."

"Nonsense," returned Molly. "When the liberties of a country like this are at stake, we should not halt at trifles. Shall we have courage, think you, to carry out my plan?"

"Yes, cried Elsie, eagerly. "Anything that can be done by mortal woman I will do—to save him."

"Once free of the sentinels, and the woods at his back, you see how easily it might be done."

"But the sentinels are alert; so are the guards."

"You forget that this is to be a holiday night. That was my thought. Your kind aunt is to send provisions enough for the whole camp, I was going to say."

"Yes, yes; I know that."

"But we must get drugged wine for the sentinels on guard, and for those about his person."

"Great heaven! Molly, would you murder them?" cried Elsie, aghast.

"By no means; only set them to sleep so soundly that they will not wake up till to-morrow morning."

"But how to get to them?"

"This way: one of the youngest of the officers is to be drugged at the party. When the wine affects him it is my duty to cajole him into another room; Joe's duty to strip him of his regimentals; your duty to put them on; the duty of all three to go to the camp—myself as a servant of Lady Walsingham—you as a Hessian officer with the pass-word—Joe with an immense hamper for the prisoner. Under the eatables is to be concealed your dress. Washburn is to exchange with you—he to put on the Hessian uniform. He is to pass out with me when the guards are sufficiently stupefied. Then you can resume your dress, and trust to your wits for getting out of the difficulty."

Elsie drew her breath hard.

"Can I do all this?" she cried.

"You said you could, just now," replied Molly.

"If we fail!"

"We shall not fail. I feel as strong as a thousand Hessians."

"You will make me brave, Molly."

"I wish to."

"It looks as if we might succeed," said Elsie, growing more hopeful.

"We are sure to."

"But what if they miss us from the party?"

"You are to complain of headache to your aunt, and ask for an hour's rest, sending your apologies to the General by her."

"Molly, you ought to be a General yourself!" cried Elsie, admiringly.

"I'd rather be a captain," said Molly, blushing.

"Well, Captain Molly, my courage is rising. If Joe only does his part well, I don't see as the rest is so very difficult."

"It is difficult," said Molly; "but, remember, he only is great who surmounts obstacles. We must face the dark, and the cold, and the danger. My only hope is its being a holiday night, and that the Hessians, filled with good cheer, will be off their guard."

"About what time is this serio-comic exhibition to commence, captain?" asked Elsie.

"The guests will be here by nine. The gentlemen will be seated at the card-tables about eleven. Then our operations must begin. I trust we shall be through by twelve."

"It is nearly time to dress," said Elsie. "How little they will guess what strange hopes and fears are going on under these costly laces," she added, moving toward the bed, where the finery was spread out. The bell rung. Molly was summoned to the boudoir of her ladyship.

"Molly," cried the latter, "Franz has disappointed me about my hair, and I do believe, after all, I must bother you to do it."

"If I can suit you," responded Molly, cheerfully.

"Of course you can, though I had set my heart upon a hair-dresser: but Franz is sick, so I must do the best I can. That's not saying, though, that you won't suit me. You've a good deal of taste for a little body."

Molly cheerfully complied. Everything was at hand—pins, dressings, pomatums, curling-irons—and she went to work with a will."

"What do you think of this story?" queried Lady Walsingham.

"What story?" asked Molly, innocently.

"Of the widow Green's son. Did you know that he came near being arrested the other day?"

"I heard something about it," said Molly, flushing.

"Look out, my little girl," said Lady Walsingham, shaking her finger at her. "Do you know they say that very same fortune-teller who came here was the man? Ah! don't tell me you didn't suspect. You are a little rebel, I'm afraid, after all, and I don't know what I shall do with you."

"And they didn't arrest him, of course?" said Molly,

hiding herself behind a handful of hair that she was holding.

"No; do you think I should like to arrest such a smart young man myself? I never heard anything like it—such a variety of disguises as he has gone into. Why, the other night, there he was right before them—had dressed himself in the girl's clothes, and so he entertained them after she had gone; next day, although they had one of the soldiers on guard, he managed it so nicely that they never suspected—got off, and the real servant came back. I call that a smart Yankee trick, don't you?"

"Very smart," said Molly, with a great relish, for she was chuckling to herself.

"Yes, no doubt you'd say so. Ah, Molly, after all my good instructions, I'm afraid you'll fail me at last."

"Why should you be?" asked Molly, again taking shelter behind the thick hair.

"Your father came here to-day, Molly."

"Father!" The girl was astonished.

"Yes; he came, he said, to have a little private talk with me."

"What! about me?" queried Molly.

"Yes, about you. It seems he is getting anxious, and wants you at home again."

"Not immediately?"

"As soon as the party is over."

"Oh!" and Molly drew a long breath of relief.

"You wouldn't like to go before, Molly?"

"I don't think I should, just as it's right upon us."

"I'm sure I don't know what I should have done without you, even if you are a little rebel; and I hope that's not very deep-seated — only for love or fancy's sake, perhaps. But your father has heard some sort of nonsense about this Captain Paul—is that his name?—and he seems to feel afraid that you will slip through his fingers some way, and marry him. Of course, if you did, he said you should never lay a finger on any of his property; and I expect your father is a very rich man, Molly."

"He is called very rich," said the girl.

"I excused you, of course, and replied that, from what I had seen, I thought there was no reason whatever for alarm. You will observe that I have never seen you in this rebel captain's company."

Molly's blush was reflected very fairly, now, in the great mirror, but the girl stooped, as she said, "Which arrow shall I put in—that tipped with ruby or the diamond?"

"Let me see," said Lady Walsingham; "ruby won't go very well with crimson. I think I'll have the diamond to-night. What beautiful bands! I really think I shall have to take you to England with me."

"Do you think of going to England?"

"Well, I suppose I must, as the fortune-teller told me I should," answered Lady Walsingham, significantly. "By the way, what do you think of Elsie?"

"Of Elsie? How do you mean?"

"Is she very unhappy in the prospect of this marriage?"

"I don't think she is very happy," Molly replied, reluctantly. "She did not like to speak of that."

"Do you know I had a singular dream about her and the General?"

"No; I should like to hear it," said Molly.

"Why, it seemed as if they were just going to be

married, when an enormous snake glided from some part of the room, coiled up the General's body, and struck him a deadly, terrible blow, just on the left temple. I declare to you I felt faint and sick when I awoke, with the thought of it."

"I don't wonder," and Molly shuddered. "I hate to dream of snakes. It seems as if they always bring trouble."

"Yes; if there is anything in dreams, I should be inclined to infer that Elsie would not marry the General, after all."

"Oh! I hope not!" said Molly, impulsively.

"And I hope not, if it can be broken with honour. Yet it seems she has been tolerably cheerful through it all."

"Your dream impresses me that she will never marry him," said Molly.

"The time draws near," was the rejoinder, "and I, for one, hope she will marry him. I see in him the elements of a good man, though, to be sure, he is a German; but, then, the Germans are pre-eminently home people, and love their families. There! what a taste you have, little Molly; I declare it is wonderful. You'll make your fortune as a hair-dresser."

"Shall I stay till you are dressed?" asked Molly.

"But you need the time yourself, now. Besides, Elsie is to be dressed, and I wish her to look particularly well to-night. Dear, dear, what trying occasions these are!"

"But I shall have plenty of time!" persisted Molly. "I had rather stay than not."

"Oh! well, then, stay and welcome. Now, would you think me forty?" she asked, laughing, as she nodded to the answering image in the glass.

"No, nor thirty," answered Molly, with sincerity; for, indeed, the harmless lady did not seem much beyond her twenties in the brilliant light that flashed upon her, when the maid had lighted the candles.

It was some time before Molly got back to Elsie, who was very leisurely dressing.

"I thought you were never coming," said the latter.

"But oh! I've something to tell you," cried Molly, and she related the dream. Elsie shuddered.

"It does seem strange," she replied, "that I myself should dream of serpents. In the temple you say the snake struck him? Indeed, I hope he is not going to be killed. I'd far rather he should live, only not as my husband," and she shuddered again.

CHAPTER XVII.

HOW THE PLOT SUCCEEDED.

A SPLENDID sight was Walsingham House before ten o'clock on Christmas night. Lights blazed from every opening and crevice, and shone far out on the dead, white snow, in glittering lines of fire. It was a fearfully cold night, but the gay groups within knew nothing of its rigours—cared for nothing but feasting and pleasure.

Elsie had made her excuse to her aunt.

"You do look pale, my child," she said. "Yes, it is wise in you to seek some rest. I will tell the General, if he misses you. Ah! you sly girl to trap my lover. Well, I forgive you—you didn't know I had set my cap for him."

"They've been drinking famously," said Molly, in a whisper, as she joined Elsie. "I've been watching them, and there's scarcely a really sober man there, thanks to the long table," and she pointed to the object in question, sparkling with decanters and goblets of glass and silver.

"There's poor little Lavoy, making believe sweet sixteen, and, oh! my dear, there's a spy, or something, in a horrible cloak. He looks frozen, too." Molly went forward to the entrance.

"Will you get this note immediately to General Rahl?" asked the man, his heavily bearded face quite pallid.

Molly took the note.

"I know just where he is;" that was all she said, and disappeared. The man went away.

"Did you give it to him?" asked Elsie on her return.

"Hush! I burned it!"

"Oh! Molly!"

"I tell you"—and Molly's now pale face and glittering eyes came close to the ear of Elsie. It was then her turn to start and grow white.

"There is no time to lose," said Molly, firmly. "Joe has done his part to perfection. He'd kill himself for me, I believe, if I was heathen enough to ask it. Go to your room. The clothes are there. Stop, Elsie, you don't understand yet about the note. That man was Black Steve, who keeps a bar down by the river, the greatest tyrant and Tory in town. There! now keep up your courage."

Hours before that, in the chill and blackness of the most bitter night of the season, Washington, with his shivering, but hopeful troops, was crossing the frozen Delaware!

A strange, wild scene it was — the few flambeaux held in the forward boats glaring in small, stolid circles, showing the broad-shouldered, heavily-bearded "Marbleheaders," sturdily managing the boats, as they made their way laboriously among the great masses of floating, cracking ice, sometimes crashing together, to the imminent danger of crushing each other. The silence, or suppressed shouts, made the scene one of solemnity as well as peril. The cutting night-air deadened the skin to the very bone, and two of the devoted men were frozen stark and stiff before the crossing was ended.

Molly had some inkling of this, but precisely how the matter was accomplished, she could not tell. The note she had burned read thus:—

"General Rahl,—A scout has arrived, who says the American Army is coming—is only nine miles away.

"FROM A FRIEND TO THE CAUSE."

Still, it did but stimulate the undaunted Molly.

"If they are surprised," she said to Elsie, "they may kill him in their anger; and if he is free, why, he will have a chance to fight in the good cause if there is any fighting to be done."

Elsie shuddered, partly with the cold, partly with a foreboding of the morrow. The prisoner safe away, she would defy the Hessian commander; but would this night's work end in victory or defeat?

As Molly had prophesied, the soldiers had had their share of Christmas-cheer, and were in a state of jollity. Elsie trembled under her military cloak, as they passed the first sentinels, and she could scarcely steady her voice to repeat the talismanic words:—

"It is daybreak."

"Pass on," was the reply.

I should have said before this, that Elsie long had been an excellent German scholar, that language being her specialty, on account of her father's strong love of it, and her ambition to master all its intricacies. The last sentinel was not so complaisant, and gruffly demanded, with a "mein Got," what they were going to feed up the rebel for ? He had already had enough.

Elsie threw aside her cloak, and no sooner did the soldier see the insignia of rank than he shrunk back cowed and quiet.

They reached the solitary house, behind which the great pines, their ghostlike arms shrouded in snow, seemed like so many weird spirits, watching over the destinies of the apparently doomed land.

The sentinels admitted them without a word—seeing a superior officer with them, who seemed to have come for the purpose of superintending the operations; while Molly took out the good cheer, and poured liberal flagons of wine for the delighted guards, who laughed heartily at her unintelligible gibberish.

The captive lieutenant-colonel at first looked moodily on—then slowly began to take in the meaning of the scene. His haggard face brightened; he cast suspicious glances toward the tall young officer, whose cap was brought low over the eyes, and who stood as much in the shadow as possible.

Wine was poured for the prisoner, cake and meat set before him. He read the dumb language expressed in the rapid motion of Molly's fingers, " Eat heartily," and obeyed.

" The guards having drank to excess, threw themselves down, thoroughly overpowered, and were soon sleeping, senselessly.

" You are to dress in that uniform," said Molly, as Elsie hurried into the next room. " Not a word—it must be done !"

"But I shall expose you all to insult and detection."

"And if you do not do as I tell you, you lose Elsie Vernon. To-morrow, to save you from the gallows, she will become the wife of General Rahl."

The prisoner grew white to the lips.

"I shall do as you say," he exclaimed, in a low voice.

At that moment Elsie came out, pale and trembling.

He grasped her hand; their eyes met in one eloquent glance.

"My glorious preserver!" he murmured, his lips quivering.

In a few moments, he, too, came out, fully equipped—all insufficiency of dress hidden by the ample cloak.

"What are you doing?" cried Elsie, as Molly threw her own cloak over her shoulders.

"You are to go with him and Joe," said Molly.

"And leave you here!" cried Elsie.

"I tell you not to think of me. Remember to-morrow. You must go with him."

"But where?" cried Elsie.

"Hist!" cried Joe, who had been watching at the entrance.

"Great God! what does it mean?" exclaimed the lieutenant-colonel.

"It means that Washington's army has crossed the Delaware," said Molly.

"The camp has heard it," cried Joe.

Nearer it sounded—the glorious old fife and drum!

"Off with the Hessian uniform!" shouted the prisoner. "There's work to do. Girls, find your way back with Joe. I can take care of myself, now."

He unbuckled the arms of the sleeping sentinel, and rapidly changed his attire.

"Good-night—God for ever bless you!" he cried, pressing Elsie to his bosom, and then dashing out into the darkness.

Tumult and confusion reigned. From what quarter the attack would come nobody knew. Half the soldiers were stupid from excessive potations, and still the shrill fife and the battle-drums drew near.

CHAPTER XVIII.
THE EVENTS OF A DAY.

BUT not yet heard at Walsingham House. There the revelry was almost wild. A full band gave forth its sonorous music—the dancers were footing it to the merriest of tunes.

"Your niece stays long," said the Hessian commander, to Lady Walsingham.

"She was very much fatigued; besides, General, she wishes, no doubt, to be bright to-morrow. However, I I will go myself and call her."

"I beg you will not," returned the General.

Nevertheless, Lady Walsingham did hurry, on the moment, to the room of her niece.

She found it in disorder—apparel scattered round, and the rich ball-dress thrown partly on the bed, partly on the floor.

Suddenly, in the midst of her consternation, Elsie entered, pale and wild, her every-day garments wet and white with the snow.

"In heaven's name, what have you been doing!" cried Lady Walsingham.

Elsie could not speak. Her tongue seemed frozen. She sunk into the first chair.

"Tell me, Elsie Vernon, what means all this? Where have you been in the night and snow? Are you mad?"

Elsie shook her head, but still felt as if all power of speech was for ever denied her.

"Elsie Vernon, I command you to answer me. What does this midnight visit from the house mean?"

"It means," cried Molly, coming in quietly, "that Miss Elsie is very tired and — very happy! The American army has crossed the Delaware; we heard the fifes and drums—oh, such a terrible army!—forty times as large as the Hessian force."

The woman grew fairly pale, with her fear and excitement.

"You wretches!" she cried, "there has been treachery here. I don't believe a word of what you say. Tell me, this instant—"

The dull thud of a single cannon at that moment smote her ear.

"I told you so," cried Molly.

Lady Walsingham flew down-stairs.

Several Hessian soldiers were elbowing their way through the gay crowds, in search of their General. Their shouts awoke consternation and terror.

"The American army is upon us—the American army has crossed the Delaware," was the cry. Men and women rushed, in frantic haste, to doors and windows. All the town was in consternation. The fife and drum could be distinctly heard in the distance. Cries and shouts were mingled in strange discord. Those who were cowardly ran, in their frantic fear, to hide themselves; others, more courageous, fled home through bye-ways.

General Rahl summoned his tipsy officers, with oaths that almost sobered them.

He rode to head-quarters, followed by his staff, and found his command prepared to surrender. His presence, however, somewhat changed the aspect of affairs, and the Hessians made ready to give battle.

The strife was a short but a bloody one. Washington rode among his soldiers, himself directing their movements. Many balls whistled by his ear—many a bullet pierced his covering cloak; but he kept his position till victory was assured.

Two hours after the defeat, an officer rode up to Washington's head-quarters.

"Lieutenant Colonel Washburn!" exclaimed the General, as he gave him his hand. "Well, I heard you were hung, or going to be."

"Alive still, General, thank God, and able to do service," responded the officer.

"Heaven be thanked that the victory is with us. Nevertheless, my reinforcements have disappointed me, and we shall not be able to hold on here."

"I am sorry for that, General."

"So am I, chiefly on account of my poor, bare-footed soldiers; but we must be wary. A few more such blows as this, and we are safe. I heard that Colonel Rahl, General by brevet, was wounded in the fight. Is that so?"

"Wounded, General, and I fear mortally."

"Ah, I'm sorry for that," said Washington. "He was a brave man. Where is he?"

"At the house of Lady Walsingham."

"I think I'll go and see him," said Washington.

Accompanied by the lieutenant-colonel, the General hurried over to the house where the Hessian commander was, indeed, dying. He had been fatally wounded.

Attended by the mistress of the house, the Hessian gazed with filming eyes where sat Elsie, white and sorrowful, while Molly was busy in some little arrangement for his comfort.

"General," said Washington, "I am sorry to meet you thus."

"And I am sorry to be met in this condition, but it is one of the casualties which must be expected in war." Again his dying eyes turned to Elsie, and he kept murmuring:—

"I see differently, now."

"Do you not wish for a clergyman?" asked Washington, who was always anxious for the spiritual condition of his friends and his enemies.

"Yes," was the brief response. "I did not, but now I do."

Lady Walsingham despatched a servant, who soon returned with a minister. Molly started and flushed as she saw enter with him Captain Paul Green.

The commander was left alone with the clergyman.

Presently the lieutenant-colonel was summoned to his bedside. He re-appeared in a few moments and spoke earnestly with Elsie.

"General Washington," he said, after his short conference, "General Rahl wishes to do what he considers an act of justice. Through motives that need not be mentioned here, he had persuaded this lady to engage herself to him. This was to have been her wedding-day. It will please him, therefore, to see her wedded to the man to whom she has long been affianced. Will you honour us by witnessing the ceremony?"

The General assented with pleasure. Elsie left the room, followed by Molly.

"Stop!" cried Captain Paul, and before Molly had time to leave he had caught her by the hand.

"Now or never," he whispered, as she turned her flushed face toward him; "now or never, if you had rather be left a widow than a forlorn maiden."

Nothing more was said by the trembling girl, and an impressive double wedding took place by the side of the dying commander.

I need only add that Molly did not become a widow, though her father cast her off. The *sobriquet* of captain always clung to her, and it it said Washington really conferred the title, in consequence of her bravery, when she accompanied her husband some time afterward.

The lieutenant was raised to the rank of a General, long before our troubles in that war were over, and distinguished himself numberless times—so that his name has come down to us full of honours.

Lady Walsingham returned to England and married again; and often, to delighted friends, she told her Christmas-night experience, and the story of Captain Molly.

THE END.

LONDON: W. J. JOHNSON, PRINTER, 121, FLEET STREET

A COMPLETE NOVEL FOR SIXPENCE!

BEADLE'S
AMERICAN SIXPENNY PUBLICATIONS.
EACH WORK ORIGINAL AND COMPLETE.

LIBRARY.

1. SETH JONES.
2. ALICE WILDE, the Raftsman's Daughter.
3. THE FRONTIER ANGEL.
4. MALAESKA.
5. UNCLE EZEKIEL.
6. MASSASOIT'S DAUGHTER.
7. BILL BIDDON, TRAPPER.
8. THE BACKWOOD'S BRIDE.
9. NATT TODD.
10. MYRA, the Child of Adoption.
11. THE GOLDEN BELT.
12. SYBIL CHASE; or, The Valley Ranche.
13. MONOWANO, the Shawnee Spy.
14. THE BRETHREN OF THE COAST.
15. KING BARNABY.
16. THE FOREST SPY.
17. THE FAR WEST.
18. RIFLEMEN OF THE MIAMI.
19. ALICIA NEWCOMBE.
20. THE HUNTER'S CABIN.
21. THE BLOCK HOUSE; or, The Wrong Man.
22. THE ALLENS.
23. ESTHER; or, The Oregon Trail.
24. RUTH MARGERIE; or, The Revolt of 1689.
25. OONOMOO, THE HURON.
26. THE GOLD HUNTERS.
27. THE TWO GUARDS.
28. SINGLE EYE, the Indians' Terror.
29. MABEL MEREDITH.
30. AHMO'S PLOT.
31. THE SCOUT.
32. THE KING'S MAN; or, Patriot and Tory.
33. KENT, THE RANGER.
34. THE PEON PRINCE.
35. IRONA.
36. LAUGHING EYES; or, The White Captive.
37. MAHASKA, the Indian Queen.
38. THE SLAVE SCULPTOR.
39. MYRTLE.
40. INDIAN JIM.
41. THE WRECKER'S PRIZE.
42. THE BRIGANTINE.
43. THE INDIAN QUEEN.
44. THE MOOSE HUNTER.
45. THE CAVE CHILD.
46. THE LOST TRAIL.
47. WRECK OF THE ALBION.
48. JOE DAVIES'S CLIENT.
49. THE CUBAN HEIRESS.
50. THE HUNTER'S ESCAPE.
51. THE SILVER BUGLE.
52. POMFRET'S WARD.
53. QUINDARO.
54. RIVAL SCOUTS.
55. THE TRAPPER'S PASS.
56. THE HERMIT.
57. THE ORONOCO CHIEF.
58. ON THE PLAINS.
59. THE SCOUT'S PRIZE.
60. RED PLUME.
61. THE THREE HUNTERS.
62. THE SECRET SHOT.

BIOGRAPHIES.

LIFE OF GARIBALDI.
LIFE OF COL. DAVID CROCKETT.
LIFE AND TIMES OF DANIEL BOONE.
KIT CARSON.
PONTIAC, THE CONSPIRATOR.
FREMONT.
LIFE OF TECUMSEH.

TALES.

THE HUNTED LIFE.
MADGE WYLDE.
HUNTING ADVENTURES IN THE NORTHERN WILDS.
THAYEN-DA-NE-GEA.
FLORIDA.
LEGENDS OF THE MISSOURI AND MISSISSIPPI. Parts I., II., III.

USEFUL LIBRARY.

READY REMEDIES FOR COMMON COMPLAINTS.
COOKERY BOOK.
RECIPE BOOK.

PRICE SIXPENCE.

London: GEORGE ROUTLEDGE & SONS, The Broadway, Ludgate Hill; and all Booksellers.

ROUTLEDGE'S
SIXPENNY HANDBOOKS.

With Illustrations, and Illustrated Boarded Covers.
(Postage 1d.)

SWIMMING AND SKATING. By the Author of "Every Boy's Book."

GYMNASTICS. By the Rev. J. G. Wood.

CHESS. With Diagrams. By G. F. Pardon.

WHIST. By G. F. Pardon.

BILLIARDS AND BAGATELLE. By Pardon.

DRAUGHTS AND BACKGAMMON. By Pardon.

CRICKET. By Edmund Routledge.

CARDPLAYER (The). By Pardon.

ROWING AND SAILING.

RIDING AND DRIVING.

ARCHERY, FENCING, AND BROADSWORD.

CONUNDRUMS.

MANLY EXERCISES: Boxing, Running, Walking, Training, &c. By Stonehenge, &c.

CROQUET. With Illustrations, Diagrams, &c. By Edmund Routledge.

GEORGE ROUTLEDGE & SONS, Broadway, Ludgate Hill.

ROUTLEDGE'S SHILLING NOVELS.

By J. FENIMORE COOPER.

In fcp. 8vo, fancy covers, 1s. each.

THE PILOT.
THE PIONEERS.
THE DEERSLAYER.
LIONEL LINCOLN.
THE BRAVO.
THE TWO ADMIRALS.
THE WATERWITCH.
WYANDOTTE.
MILES WALLINGFORD.
THE PRAIRIE.
THE HEATHCOTES.
PRECAUTION.
MARK'S REEF.
THE LAST OF THE MOHICANS.
THE SPY.
THE PATHFINDER.
THE RED ROVER.
THE HEIDENMAUER.
SATANSTOE.
AFLOAT AND ASHORE.
EVE EFFINGHAM.
THE HEADSMAN.
HOMEWARD BOUND.
THE SEA LIONS.
OAK OPENINGS.
NED MYERS.

GEORGE ROUTLEDGE & SONS, Broadway, Ludgate Hill.

ROUTLEDGE'S SHILLING NOVELS.

By W. HARRISON AINSWORTH.

WINDSOR CASTLE.

THE MISER'S DAUGHTER.

THE TOWER OF LONDON.

CRICHTON.

JAMES THE SECOND.

OLD ST. PAUL'S.

THE FLITCH OF BACON.

GUY FAWKES.

THE LANCASHIRE WITCHES.

MERVYN CLITHEROE.

OVINGDEAN GRANGE.

ROOKWOOD.

ST. JAMES'S; OR, THE COURT OF QUEEN ANNE.

THE SPENDTHRIT.

THE STAR CHAMBER.

AURIOL.

JACK SHEPPARD.

GEORGE ROUTLEDGE & SONS, Broadway, Ludgate Hill.

ROUTLEDGE'S SHILLING NOVELS.

By G. P. R. JAMES.

In fcp. 8vo, fancy covers, 1s. each.

THE BRIGAND.
DARNLEY.
THE WOODMAN.
MORLEY ERNSTEIN.
THE GIPSY.
HENRY OF GUISE.
ATTILA.
ARABELLA STUART.
AGINCOURT.
RUSSELL; OR, THE RYE HOUSE PLOT.
THE KING'S HIGHWAY.
THE CASTLE OF EHRENSTEIN.
THE STEPMOTHER.
FOREST DAYS; OR, ROBIN HOOD.
THE HUGUENOT.
THE MAN AT ARMS.
A WHIM AND ITS CONSEQUENCES.
HENRY MASTERTON.
THE CONVICT.
MARY OF BURGUNDY.
MARGARET GRAHAM.
GOWRIE; OR, THE KING'S PLOT.
DELAWARE.
DARK SCENES OF HISTORY.
THE ROBBER.
ONE IN A THOUSAND.
THE SMUGGLER.
RICHELIEU.
DE LORME.
ARRAH NEIL.
BEAUCHAMP.
CASTELNEAU.
THE FALSE HEIR.
THE FORGERY.
THE GENTLEMAN OF THE OLD SCHOOL.
HEIDELBERG.
THE JACQUERIE.
MY AUNT PONTYPOOL
ROSE D'ALBRET.
SIR THEODORE BROUGHTON.
CHARLES TYRRELL.
JOHN MARSTON HALL.
PHILIP AUGUSTUS.
THE BLACK EAGLE.
LEONORA D'ORCO.
THE OLD DOMINION.

GEORGE ROUTLEDGE & SONS, Broadway, Ludgate Hill.

ROUTLEDGE'S SHILLING NOVELS.

By CAPTAIN MARRYAT.

In fscp. 8vo, fancy covers, 1s. each.

- PETER SIMPLE.
- JACOB FAITHFUL.
- NEWTON FORSTER.
- THE PACHA OF MANY TALES.
- PERCIVAL KEENE.
- JAPHET IN SEARCH OF A FATHER.
- FRANK MILDMAY.
- MR. MIDSHIPMAN EASY.
- THE POACHER.
- VALERIE.
- THE KING'S OWN.
- RATTLIN THE REEFER.
- THE PHANTOM SHIP.
- THE DOG FIEND.

MISCELLANEOUS.

1s. each.

- NOTHING BUT MONEY. By T. S. ARTHUR.
- THE FAMILY FEUD. By THOMAS COOPER.
- ADELAIDE LINDSAY. By the Author of "EMILIA WYNDHAM."
- THE LITTLE WIFE. By Mrs. GREY.
- RITA: An AUTOBIOGRAPHY.
- LILLY DAWSON. By Mrs. CROWE.
- THE HENPECKED HUSBAND. By LADY SCOTT.
- WHOM TO MARRY. By MAYHEW.
- TOUGH YARNS. By the "OLD SAILOR."

GEORGE ROUTLEDGE & SONS, Broadway, Ludgate Hill.

JAMES GRANT'S NOVELS.

Price 2s. each, in Fancy Boards.

THE ROMANCE OF WAR; or, The Highlanders in Spain.

THE AIDE-DE-CAMP.

THE SCOTTISH CAVALIER.

BOTHWELL.

JANE SETON; or, The Queen's Advocate.

PHILIP ROLLO.

LEGENDS OF THE BLACK WATCH.

MARY OF LORRAINE.

OLIVER ELLIS; or, The Fusiliers.

LUCY ARDEN; or, Hollywood Hall.

FRANK HILTON; or, The Queen's Own.

THE YELLOW FRIGATE.

HARRY OGILVIE; or, The Black Dragoons.

ARTHUR BLANE.

LAURA EVERINGHAM; or, The Highlanders of Glenora.

THE CAPTAIN OF THE GUARD.

LETTY HYDE'S LOVERS.

CAVALIERS OF FORTUNE.

SECOND TO NONE.

THE CONSTABLE OF FRANCE.

The above in Cloth Gilt, 2s. 6d. each.

GEORGE ROUTLEDGE & SONS, Broadway, Ludgate Hill.

LORD LYTTON'S WORKS.

CHEAP EDITION, in fscp. 8vo, Boards,

Price 2s. each.

A STRANGE STORY.
WHAT WILL HE DO WITH IT? Vol. I.
WHAT WILL HE DO WITH IT? Vol. II.
PELHAM.
PAUL CLIFFORD.
EUGENE ARAM.
THE LAST DAYS OF POMPEII.
THE LAST OF THE BARONS.
RIENZI.
ERNEST MALTRAVERS.
ALICE.
NIGHT AND MORNING.
THE DISOWNED.
DEVEREUX.
THE CAXTONS.
MY NOVEL. Vol. I.
MY NOVEL. Vol. II.
LUCRETIA.
HAROLD.

Price 1s. 6d. each.

GODOLPHIN. | ZANONI.

Price 1s. each.

THE PILGRIMS OF THE RHINE.
LEILA; OR, THE SIEGE OF GRANADA.

GEORGE ROUTLEDGE & SONS, Broadway, Ludgate Hill.

www.ingramcontent.com/pod-product-compliance
Lightning Source LLC
Chambersburg PA
CBHW021939160426
43195CB00011B/1158